Social Issues
in Literature

Death and Dying
in the Poetry
of Emily Dickinson

Other Books in the Social Issues in Literature Series:

Social Issues
in Literature

Death and Dying
in the Poetry
of Emily Dickinson

Claudia Durst Johnson, Book Editor

GREENHAVEN PRESS
A part of Gale, Cengage Learning

GALE
CENGAGE Learning·

Detroit • New York • San Francisco • New Haven, Conn • Waterville, Maine • London

Elizabeth Des Chenes, *Director, Publishing Solutions*

© 2013 Greenhaven Press, a part of Gale, Cengage Learning

Gale and Greenhaven Press are registered trademarks used herein under license.

For more information, contact:
Greenhaven Press
27500 Drake Rd.
Farmington Hills, MI 48331-3535
Or you can visit our Internet site at gale.cengage.com

For product information and technology assistance, contact us at

Gale Customer Support, 1-800-877-4253
For permission to use material from this text or product, submit all requests online at www.cengage.com/permissions

Further permissions questions can be emailed to permissionrequest@cengage.com

Articles in Greenhaven Press anthologies are often edited for length to meet page requirements. In addition, original titles of these works are changed to clearly present the main thesis and to explicitly indicate the author's opinion. Every effort is made to ensure that Greenhaven Press accurately reflects the original intent of the authors. Every effort has been made to trace the owners of copyrighted material.

Cover image © Lebrecht Music and Arts Photo Library/Alamy.

LIBRARY OF CONGRESS CATALOGING-IN-PUBLICATION DATA

Death and dying in the poetry of Emily Dickinson / Claudia Durst Johnson, book editor.
      p. cm. -- (Social issues in literature)
   Includes bibliographical references and index.
   ISBN 978-0-7377-6375-1 (hardcover) -- ISBN 978-0-7377-6376-8 (pbk.)
   1. Dickinson, Emily, 1830-1886--Criticism and interpretation. 2. Death in literature.
   PS1541.Z5D43 2012
   811'.4--dc23
                                                            2012007815

Printed in Mexico
2 3 4 5 6 7 16 15 14 13 12

Contents

Chapter 3: Contemporary Perspectives on Death and Dying

Introduction

The last half of the twentieth century and the early decades of the twenty-first century have seen the proliferation of youthful countercultures obsessed with death in somewhat attention-getting fads. The goths have been most prominent with their dramatic black clothing, black hair, black lipstick and mascara. Their symbols are death related, such as vampires, ghosts, skulls, and funerary art. One of the characteristic activities of goths is to wander through graveyards. A similar subculture is centered on the rock music genre called emo (short for "emotional hardcore"). Many of its fans (called emos) irresponsibly romanticize suicide, which has resulted in trajedies among troubled and naive teens. Both goths and emos as well as teenage culture in general have been bombarded with popular films and novels about grotesque and supernatural death.

Although the young goths of the twenty-first century are separated from Emily Dickinson by approximately eighteen decades, a literary movement of the late eighteenth and early nineteenth centuries, also fixated on death, inspired them both. These were the English gothic novels and plays that quickly and permanently became absorbed into American culture though they are not usually a part of the literary canon. These novels are replete with ghosts, violent murders, the living dead, tombs, crypts, skeletons, and corpses. The primary gothic novels, rife with terror, are Mrs. Radcliffe's *The Mysteries of Udolpho* (1794); Matthew Lewis's *The Monk* (1797), about grotesque and rotting corpses; Mary Shelley's *Frankenstein* (1817), a horror story of a man-made monster who turns on humans; and Charles Maturin's *Melmoth the Wanderer* (1820), about the pain of a life without death. Bram Stoker's 1897 *Dracula*, the death-bringing vampire, has become an icon of the present-day goths but did not appear, of course, until eleven years after Dickinson's death.

Emily Dickinson was influenced primarily not only by gothic novels but, more importantly, by the reality of death all around her. In her society she was not alone in her morbidity, for deaths occurred with unsettling frequency in the nineteenth century. The average life expectancy has been estimated to be somewhere around forty years old. Deaths of women in childbirth were constant reminders of mortality. And it was a rare family who did not lose an infant at birth in a time when families had between ten and twelve children. Some have estimated that as many as 25 percent of infants were born dead or died shortly after. Many children were lost to fatal diseases, accidents, fires, and natural disasters, which also took the lives of adults in great numbers as well. Sociologists have attributed the emotional distance that parents often maintained from their children, to the parents' desire to lessen the trauma should their offspring die.

As historians Barton Levi St. Armand and Ann Douglass have pointed out, the plethora of children's deaths resulted in the image of the child being made the chief emblem in much literature and art. So many deaths radically changed the old Calvinist view of children being born depraved and doomed to an outer circle of hell, because they had not the opportunity to be justified.

Instead, under the influence of romantics like Ralph Waldo Emerson, children came to be viewed as innocents.

Dickinson's world was also traumatized by the untimely deaths of young men during the American Civil War, a subject which often enters her poetry. An estimated half a million soldiers died in the war.

Her society's fascination with death gave rise to overwhelming amounts of cemetery art, often paintings or sketches of a tombstone draped by a willow tree with a mourning maiden beside it.

As St. Armand points out, the extremes to which individuals went in their constant romanticism of death inspired Mark Twain to parody the death-obsessive art of the time in *Huckleberry Finn* in 1884/1885. Emmeline Grangerford, a character in that book, in a maudlin hysteria, frantically wrote shallow rhymed verses as fast as she could, upon getting word of someone's death. It was a matter of great pride to her that her poem mourning a dead person preceded the appearance of the undertaker. She dropped dead upon one occasion when the undertaken got there first.

The issue of death is integral to any society. In Dickinson's day it left children without mothers. It tore apart families by taking away fathers who supported them. It severed deep emotional ties. And, no matter how humble or extravagant the monument, death reminded the living that death was a leveler. A wealthy man was just as dead as a poor one.

Equally important was the impact of death's reality on the religious faith of a community. Death fortified most people in their beliefs in God and in an afterlife, a place where they would be reunited with loved ones. Faith satisfied them that their loved one died for a reason, usually rationalized by saying that God wanted the loved one to be with Him, or that death terminated suffering, or even that the person who had "passed on" was bad and the world was better off without him or that death was punishment for the sins of the family.

On the other hand, some few, like Emily Dickinson, found their faith challenged by death. How could a just God take away a beloved young person? What reason had we to believe they lived on after the finality of death? These were questions she raised but never seems to have resolved.

The following excerpts from criticism are divided into three chapters: death in Emily Dickinson's life; death in her poetry; and contemporary issues involving death. The first chapter explores her biography, the effect of the many deaths of friends and acquaintances in her young life, and the psychological explanation for her obsession with death.

The second chapter is an exploration of varied issues that arise in her poems on death. These include how the subject of death stimulated her imagination, how death is the unraveling of a final mystery or the securing of ultimate freedom or adventure. Her poems also delve into the pain of the grieving and her conflicting views of God and immortality.

The third chapter examines contemporary considerations of death: dealing with grief, facing one's own certain death, and humane ways of dealing with the dying.

Chronology

December 10, 1830

Emily Elizabeth Dickinson is born in Amherst, Massachusetts.

May–June, 1844

Dickinson's childhood friend dies and Dickinson is sent to visit relatives in Boston.

September 1847

She enters Mount Holyoke Female Seminary.

August 1848

She undergoes a religious crisis and withdraws from Mount Holyoke.

January 1850

Leonard Humphrey, one of her friends and mentors dies.

1850–1875

Dickinson publishes poems in magazines.

March 24, 1853

A close friend, Ben Newton dies.

March 1855

She meets one of the greatest influences on her life, the Reverend Charles Wadsworth, a poet who will maintain a correspondence with her and visit her several times.

1858–1861

Dickinson has a mysterious correspondence with someone with whom she was in love and who remains unidentified.

Winter and Spring 1862

Dickinson suffers what appears to be a mental breakdown. She writes 366 poems this year and begins corresponding with Thomas Wentworth Higginson, a literary figure who will also visit her in Amherst. She becomes increasingly confined to the bedroom of her house.

June 16, 1874

Her father dies and she befriends Judge Otis P. Lord, with whom she has a romantic relationship.

June 28, 1877

Dickinson is visited by another literary mentor, Samuel Bowles.

January 16, 1878

Samuel Bowles dies.

April 1, 1882

The Reverend Wadsworth dies. In November of this year her mother dies.

October 5, 1883

Dickinson's favorite nephew dies at the age of nine.

March 15, 1884

Judge Otis dies.

May 15, 1886

Emily Dickinson dies. After her death, her sister, Lavinia, discovers 1,775 of Emily's 1,789 poems. At Dickinson's request, Lavinia destroys the letters Emily had saved.

1890 and 1891

Two volumes of her poetry are published.

November 21, 1894
Two volumes of Dickinson's letters are published.

Background on
Emily Dickinson

The Life of Emily Dickinson

Ruth Miller

Ruth Miller, scholar and former professor at Stony Brook, is the author of The Poetry of Emily Dickinson *and* The Myth of Amherst.

Miller explains in the following excerpt that Dickinson, whose poems are recognized now as precursors of modern poetry, failed miserably in getting her poems published. She wrote more than 1,500 poems for which manuscripts exist. Only a handful were published in her lifetime. She was born into a prominent family in Amherst, Massachusetts; made friends at Amherst Academy, where she was schooled; and, for a year, attended what is now Mount Holyoke College. Between 1858 and 1862 she suffered some kind of mental trauma. Her eccentricities included secluding herself in her father's house; at some point, isolating herself in her room; and always dressing in white. The important people in her life were her father and mother; her brother Austin and his wife, Susan; her sister Lavinia; a newspaper editor named Samuel Bowles; and a literary editor, Thomas Wentworth Higginson. Though Higginson never published any of her poems, he continued to serve as her literary mentor.

To be a poet was the sole ambition of Emily Dickinson. She achieved what she called her immortality by total commitment to the task, allowing nothing to deter her or intervene. Contrary to the myth that she would not deign to publish her verse, she made herculean efforts to reach out to a world that was not ready for the poems she offered her manner and form were fifty years ahead of her time. . . .

To be understood and appreciated, Emily Dickinson had to wait until a major shift in sensibility and expectation occurred in the decade surrounding World War I, When Imagism, a new school of poetry—precise, stripped of all extraneous verbiage, indifferent to traditional form and content, reaching always for the radical and original image and wholly unsentimental—had established itself, preparing the way for modern American poetry. . . .

Dickinson's Eccentricities

Because the biography of Emily Dickinson is so closely bound up with the meaning and substance of her poetry, a narrative of the events of her life illuminates not only her character and personality, but her poems. Bearing in mind her tendency of self-dramatization and hyperbole, we must read the letters and poems with caution, aware that while she strives to tell the truth, she always tells it "slant." However, there are facts we can be certain of, although much remains mysterious. We know she suffered a traumatic experience between the years of 1858 and 1862, but *what* that was, and whether it took the form of a single event or a cumulative series, leading to a sense of loss or failure or rejection, we cannot prove. We know she withdrew into her father's house and for the last seventeen years of her life did not venture beyond the bounds of the "Homestead" with its conservatory and spacious grounds, but *why*, whether out of bitterness, pride, fear, personality maladjustment, or sickness of soul, we are unable, finally, to say. We know she dressed in white but cannot identify the precise meaning of the symbolic color it may have meant the robe of the martyr, the garment of the virgin, or the mantle of the poet, or all three. She hid from visitors, refused to enter her brother's house, "a hedge away," for fifteen years, until the sudden illness of her beloved nephew brought her sadly to that bedside, but what caused the rupture is conjecture; we do not know if it was a quarrel or a betrayal, whether it was their choice or hers. We know she wrote over 1,500 poems because we have her manuscripts. We know she copied and recopied 863 of them until they seemed to her perfect, and tied them together into forty-three separate collections called "fascicles," which she placed into her bureau drawer for posterity to find. . . .

Dickinson's Family and Friends

What little is known of her life may be summarized briefly. Emily was born into a household that stood at the center of culture and social activity of Amherst. Her grandfather was the founder of Amherst College; her father, and later her brother, served as the treasurer of that institution for a span of fifty-nine years. Her father, Edward, was a practicing lawyer and well-known, influential public figure. . . .

Emily's mother was a simple woman, wholly dedicated to her home and family, cheerfully undertaking her domestic duties. After her husband's death she had a stroke and lingered on until 1882, an invalid under the constant care of her daughters. Emily's brother Austin was less respected than his father. Although he, too, practiced law, he was more interested in art and theater, little concerned with politics, but dedicated to the community and the college, though he chafed under the limitations imposed on him by the small town. When he married Susan Gilbert, daughter of a tavern keeper in Amherst, Emily was thrilled to have her dear friend as a sister-in-law. The newlyweds wished to go to Chicago to start a new life, but Mr. Dickinson prevailed on them to stay, building a house next door to the Homestead, and made Austin a partner in his law firm. The marriage soured early and there was always an atmosphere of tension and emotional instability in "The Evergreens." Susan was a social climber and thought of herself as the hostess of Amherst. To her house came Wendell Phillips and [Ralph Waldo] Emerson, Samuel Bowles, the editor of the *Springfield Republican*, Judge Otis P. Lord of Salem, Dr. Josiah

Portrait of the prolific, posthumously appreciated American poet Emily Dickinson, in her customary all-white dress. © Bettmann/Corbis.

Holland, the founder and editor of *Scribner's Magazine*. Bowles and Holland became life-long friends of Emily. . . .

Lavinia, Emily's younger sister, was not a profound companion but a forthright, active person with a sharp tongue, amiable enough, and practical—even a gadabout compared to

Emily. As Austin and Emily succumbed to psychological distress, Lavinia seemed to grow stronger and thrive despite her own disappointment at not being able to find a young man who would marry her. She, too, remained a spinster, and it was Lavinia who was utterly fanatical about having Emily's poems published after her death.

A few good-hearted girls, children of college faculty members, or of people well established in the town, were Emily's friends, joining with her in the usual round of parties, visits, excursions, going to the same school, and later, sustaining long correspondences. There is little comparable here to the famous friendships that existed between Emerson and [Henry David] Thoreau, [Herman] Melville and [Nathaniel] Hawthorne, William Dean Howells and Mark Twain, or Howells and [Henry] James. But her friends saved her letters, and supplied recollections of a loving but demure, shy, and self-demeaning young woman. From her "secret sharing" we begin to find traces of alienation; at first a merely wistful sense of deprivation, carrying hints of a growing discomfort about the religious conversions that were going on about her, gradually darkening into a concern with death and longings for a fulfillment that was denied to her.

Her friendships with the young men of the town were conventional transient affairs—the students or young instructors or law clerks paid court for a time and moved on. There was no fulfilling love affair. She stayed close to home, reading, working in her garden, doing chores, and writing her poetry. There is evidence that the young law student, Ben Newton, encouraged her to become a poet. He died in 1853, which enables us to come close to an early dating of the budding career. The 1850s began as a time of diversions, innocent and ordinary; they conclude with a withdrawn and isolated poet living in growing solitude. The decade started with conventional friendships and ended with the traumatic relationship with Samuel Bowles, whom she first met in 1858.

Emily had long made it a practice to send a poem to friends and relatives, tucked inside a letter, hoping it would clarify a point she could not adequately express in prose. Fifty-one poems have been found among the papers of Samuel Bowles and there is no way to tell how many more he received, how many were lost. Her letters to him show an undying hope that he would print one in his newspaper, but he refused. She brooded deeply over his indifference to her verse, noting he easily admitted to the literary columns the sentimental prattle of young lady poets Emily knew she transcended in every way. It never occurred to her that that was precisely why he could not print her verse; he himself did not fully understand her poems, and was far more interested in politics, in good food and strong drink, in glamorous women. . . .

Literary Rejection

It is unpleasant to realize the degree to which Emily Dickinson suffered at the rejection of Bowles, but she was a vulnerable woman, albeit an invulnerable poet. Asking for advice, never taking it, asking for assessment, never believing it, she wrote many wistful, pleading, wry, ironic, sorrowful letters with poems to match. They show a changing relationship from supplication to challenge to suffering and despair. She talked of her fear of death, her doubts of salvation, at the same time confessing her great longings to be recognized as a poet, revealing her absolute conviction that she had a supreme gift. . . .

On 7 July 1860, an article appeared in the *Springfield Republican* which Emily construed as a public rebuke and a rejection of all her hopes. Bowles calls attention to "the literature of misery," saying that the writers are "chiefly women . . . lonely and unhappy, whose suffering is seldom healthful." He advises them to wait until the storm is passed: "write not from the fullness of a present sorrow." Their poems reveal "a countenance we would gladly brighten, but not by exposing it to the gaze of a worthless world." It became at last apparent to Emily Dickinson there was no more to be hoped for from this quarter.

In the *Atlantic Monthly* for April 1862, she read "Letter to a Young Contributor," written by Thomas Wentworth Higginson, the literary editor, and well-known essayist. The article contained advice to poets, suggesting what they should write about, how they should train themselves, what proper style should be, and so on. At once, Dickinson sent four poems to ask his opinion of her work: "Are you too deeply occupied to say if my Verse is alive?" Higginson was gallant enough to write a reply but advised her not to publish. A correspondence ensued, twenty-two poems coming to the new mentor in the first year, and 102 others during her lifetime. She pretends to be unschooled, pretends she is a novice, humble, a willing pupil, and elevates Higginson to the role of preceptor. At no point does he seem ever to have altered his first assessment of her "effusions," as he called them. He was gentle in his counsel that she study the craft, but inflexible, refusing always to sponsor a single one of her poems.

It was about this time that Emily Dickinson withdrew from the world, into a Paradise of her own making, where she occupied herself with the writing of poems to prove to herself again and again that her mentors were wrong. . . .

Her Literary Career Removed from the World

She withdrew into the confines of her house and garden to fulfill her self-appointed mission, working on her poetry—endlessly revising, rewriting, sharpening her observations, and refining the verses. Inside the small room which held a few pieces of furniture—an iron bed, a small writing table, a painted chair, and a bureau in which she stored her finished work—she allowed her imagination to drift through her window, to wander on vast meadows, climb slopes and mountain peaks, sail on turbulent seas, and soar beyond the skies into the heavens. . . .

Her themes grew more profound, feeding on the visions she had of truths that went far beyond what she had been taught during her brief schooling at Amherst Academy between 1841 and 1847 and the curtailed year at Mount Holyoke in 1848. . . .

The career of Emily Dickinson was without further event. Higginson visited once and found the experience too draining to repeat. She refused medical care when she began to have fainting spells toward the end of her life, saying the doctor might look in on her from the doorway of her bedroom, but that was all. She died of Bright's disease [a historical classification for different types of kidney disease] on 15 May 1886. Higginson came to her funeral, and it was to him that Lavinia turned, with her young friend, Mrs. Mabel Loomis Todd, to ask for his help in the projected publication of Emily's poems.

Death and Dying Surrounded Emily Dickinson

Alfred Habegger

Alfred Habegger, formerly a professor at the University of Kansas, is now an independent scholar living in Oregon. He has written extensively on Henry James, the writer, and James's father, the scholar.

In the following excerpt, Habegger notes that Emily Dickinson's loss of traditional religious faith came after a series of deaths of people well known in the community. The windows at the back of the Dickinson house presented a daily view of the Amherst graveyard, a constant reminder of death and dying, and deaths were persistent in the area. One woman wrote, "People are always dying here." What was called the "season of dying" began in Amherst in 1842 with the deaths of two children, a four-year-old girl and a young boy. This seems to have brought on the young Dickinson's childhood crisis. Between 1843 and 1844 came the deaths of several women in the community, mothers of Dickinson's friends. At fifteen she saw her friend and cousin die. Finally, in April 1844, a friend of the family killed herself, provoking a prolonged social and personal debate about whether a woman who had taken her own life could possibly attain salvation.

"The child's faith is new" (Fr701), a poem Dickinson wrote in her early thirties, when she could feel that her innocence was finally gone, concerns the childish assumption

Alfred Habegger, *My Wars Are Laid Away in Books: The Life of Emily Dickinson*. New York: Random House, 2001. Copyright © 2001 by Alfred Habegger. Reproduced by permission of Random House, Inc. in the United Kingdom by the author. Incorporated Emily Dickinson poems from *The Poems of Emily Dickinson*, The Belknap Press of Harvard University Press. Copyright © 1951, 1955, 1979, 1983 by the President and Fellows of Harvard College. Reproduced by permission of the publishers and Trustees of Amherst College.

that paradise is attainable in a very mundane world. Behind the poem was her memory of the very great risks she had taken as a girl, when her precocious ability in approved endeavors and her responsiveness to what was set before her as vital and ultimate, especially in evangelical religion, exposed her to major inner trouble. Like Icarus, she aimed for the sun as soon as she could fly. Like his father, Daedalus, she contrived to save herself, preserving her early idealism through substitutes and compensations, postponing the crash till age thirty. Still, even this most resourceful of children was not prepared for her first season of death. . . .

Death All Around the Child

In 1882, after Dickinson's mother and father were dead, she noted that "no Verse in the Bible has frightened me so much from a Child as 'from him that hath not, shall be taken even that he hath.' Was it because its dark menace deepened our own Door?"

At first glance, these words seem to indicate an immediate fear for the members of her family, an anxiety stemming from her parents' extreme protectiveness. No doubt the girl felt that, yet we should note that the Bible verse could not have applied to the Dickinsons, who suffered no bereavements: none of *them* was "taken." In fact, the verb is "deepened," not "darkened"—a hint that death was outside the home and that it was others' losses that gave Emily a scared sense of living behind a well-fortified door. To look out and see how *catching* death proved was to experience a peculiar fear in one's protected state.

Since Amherst's burial ground was behind the Dickinsons' home on West Street, death deepened the young poet's windows as well as her doors and gates. Once, as she sat writing a friend, she broke her flow of thought to say, "I have just seen a funeral procession go by of a negro baby." Still, the casualness with which she mentioned this and other interments shows they were an aspect of community life for her, something she took for granted much as anyone else. She was not Mark Twain's Emmeline Grangerford, composing a lugubrious tribute whenever anyone died.

But of course some deaths struck nearer than others. On May 19, 1842, Lavinia and Loring Norcross lost their first child, a four-year-old girl, probably in Boston. Since the surviving letters from that spring predate the death, we know nothing about its attendant circumstances. Given the family's close ties to the Dickinsons, however, we can take for granted it was deeply felt on West Street.

At the time, careful attention was paid to last words and acts, especially in orthodox communities like Amherst. In fall 1842, after Emily Fowler's small brother died of a fever, his desolated mother sent a friend a detailed account of his last delirium. The boy had been convinced he "was in a deep well & *always* away from his pleasant home & dear parents." When given a glass of water, he thought it "was a hatchet uplifted to destroy him." At the end, when he was unable to speak and even to "see us," his tortured mother made one last effort to break through: "if Webster loves his mother press her hand." And he was just able to do so. One would like to know whether this striking deathbed story was communicated to young Emily.

"People *always* are dying here," wrote Mary Shepard in September 1843, expressing the strong sense of mortality that oppressed Amherst's inhabitants at the time. But 1843 was nothing compared to the first half of 1844, when a series of deaths made a dramatic impression on the town and precipitated the poet's most serious childhood crisis.

The Death of Her Friends' Mothers

Deborah Fiske, the gifted and vibrant wife of a professor, was remembered as one who greeted children "with a kind remark always." A victim of consumption, she had a "deep and hoarse"

Portrait of Emily Dickinson, circa 1850. Though only around twenty years old in this portrait, Dickinson had already experienced the deaths of many friends and family members. © Hulton Archive/Getty Images.

cough, weighed seventy-nine pounds by August 1843, and, aware that she was dying, kept her older daughter, Helen [Hunt Jackson], home from school. Anxious about her younger daughter, Ann, who had lost weight from illness, despondency, and loneliness, she counted on giving the nine-year-old a cheerful birthday party on December 25. Instead, she had to send a peremptory last-minute request to Emily Norcross Dickinson: "If convenient to you, Ann may visit Emily and Lavinia this afternoon . . . I had intended to let her invite your daughters and two or three other misses . . . but I am too feeble to [hear? bear?] any noise of playing."

Emily probably attended Mrs. Fiske's funeral on February 21, 1844, and heard the sermon delivered by Heman Humphrey, president of the college. Sharing the general admiration of the deceased, he took as his theme the importance of the "domestic virtues" in wives and mothers. At the end, as was the custom, he solemnly drew attention to the various classes of survivors, particularly "the bereaved children," whose "loss is far greater than they can at present realize." No one is quite so pitiable, he grimly stated, as the child "who has not enjoyed the earliest teaching, as well as caresses of a pious and faithful mother. The loss cannot be repaired." As if to qualify this dark forecast, he invoked the dead woman's spirit as his unseen listener: "I seem at this moment to see her finger upon her lips, warning me that my words should be few, and carefully chosen. I stand before God; in what other invisible presences I know not." Even if Emily missed this tremendous ghostly scene, in which choosing the right words carried so much weight, she could have read the published text after the widower presented it to her mother.

Next came the turn of Harriet W. Fowler, daughter of Noah Webster, best friend of Mrs. Fiske, wife of another professor, and mother of Webster and Emily Fowler. Harriet had also been dwindling from consumption for many years, doing her best to spare her children and make her home cheerful and hospitable. One winter night, as she lay in bed with no lamps lit, she felt her mouth filling with blood. If she got up to spit, she feared, she would have a paroxysm of coughing and wake her husband and children, so she made herself swallow "two or three mouthsful." On February 16, 1844, Mrs. Fowler was taken by sleigh to visit Mrs. Fiske, who exclaimed, "Why, how quick you breathe! Perhaps you will follow me next winter, and I shall be the first to welcome you [in heaven]." They knew this was their last sight of each other, and when the visitor tried to leave, she was called back for "another affectionate farewell." Three days later Mrs. Fiske died. Another six weeks and Mrs. Fowler followed, her suffering reportedly "severe." "Death is doing his work thoroughly in this place," observed Jeremiah Taylor, who dismissed the academy early on the afternoon of April 2 so that those who wished could attend the funeral. Chances are, Emily did and thus heard President Humphrey praise Mrs. Fowler's "sprightly conversation, cultivated manners, and refined sensibility," and also "the ceaseless overflowing of her maternal love." The Last Interview of Mrs. Fowler and Mrs. Fiske would be remembered with admiration.

Ann and Helen Fiske and Emily Fowler were not Emily's closest friends, but it was a fearful thing to see acquaintances lose a mother. The Fowler girl had to withdraw from school in order to take charge of her father's household. When another friend, Luthera Norton, lost her mother the following year, Emily reported that "she seems to feel very lonely, now her mother is dead, and thinks were she only alive it would be all she would ask. I pity her much, for she loved her mother devotedly."

The Death of Her Friend

In April came the devastating death. Sophia Holland was Emily's second cousin, a granddaughter of the Lucinda Dickinson who moved to Tennessee after lending Samuel Fowler Dickinson too much money. What little we know about the girls' friendship dates from 1846, two years later, when Emily recalled Sophia as a "friend near my age & with whom my thoughts & her own were the same." We note the resemblance between this perfect communion and what Emily had enjoyed following her conversion, and also that the cousin was two and a half years older. Her death from typhus on April 29 proved utterly traumatic. Emily was allowed to watch "over her bed," but when the dying girl grew delirious the young visitor was excluded on doctor's orders. "It seemed to me I should die too," Emily recalled, "if I could not be permitted to watch over her or even to look at her face."

On the night of April 28, a Sunday, Lucius Boltwood informed a correspondent that "Seneca Holland's daughter is very sick with a brain fever—& it is thought that she will not live till morning." It may have been that night or the next day that Emily prevailed on the doctor to allow one last look. She took off her shoes and quietly stepped to the sickroom, stopping in the doorway. There Sophia

> lay mild & beautiful as in health & her pale features lit up with an unearthly—smile. I looked as long as friends would permit & when they told me I must look no longer I let them lead me away.

The hushed calm, the bystander's rapt gaze, the uncanny and uninterpretable "smile" (the preceding dash evoking the pause in which the writer scans for the right word): this is fifteen-year-old Emily's retrospective narration of *her* first Last Interview. . . .

Letting herself be led away before she had finished looking, Emily could neither observe the moment of death nor settle the meaning of that . . . smile. Recalling the disturbing experience two years later, the girl brought into play the therapeutic formulas of her era:

> I shed no tear, for my heart was too full to weep, but after she was laid in her coffin & I felt I could not call her back again I gave way to a fixed melancholy.

I told no one the cause of my grief, though it was gnawing at my very heart strings. I was not well & I went to Boston & stayed a month & my health improved so that my spirits were better. . . .

Suicide

But there was one more death to be absorbed in 1844, the most horrifying yet. The letters sent to Emily in Boston, running from May 19 to June 4, imply she was back in Amherst at the end of June, when Martha Dwight Strong, the sixty-two-year-old wife of Hezekiah Wright Strong, a prominent man who had often figured in the Dickinson family's annals, killed herself. According to the *Hampshire Gazette*, Mrs. Strong had been both incoherent and depressed of late, frequently declaring "she should soon give up the Ghost." On Sunday, the thirtieth, apparently "quite cheerful," she was left at home while her husband went to church. Unable to find her on his return, he "at last discovered her in a well in the yard," into which she had apparently "thrown herself headlong." The official death notice gives the cause of death as "Suicide. Drowned in a state of mental derangement."

In general, suicides were not considered eligible for heaven. But *was* Mrs. Strong's death a suicide if she wasn't in her right mind? And who is to say the all-powerful God of John Calvin cannot raise up such a person if He so elects? . . .

Only after Father's death, when "sacred" things enlarged and "dim" things were recovered, was Dickinson ready to bring this memory up from the Strongs' fearsome well. . . .

What the young listener surmised was that God might be weaker than he was thought to be and that heaven could be a fable—two more burdensome issues not to be carried to Mother or Father and thus necessitating a further increase in her own powers. As she would one day write,

I can wade Grief—
Whole Pools of it—
I'm used to that. . .
Fr312

Dickinson's Obsession with Death

John Cody

John Cody, an authority on Emily Dickinson, worked as a psychiatrist until 1986, when he began to devote himself to a career as a painter. His art is known worldwide.

Cody takes a psychological approach to Dickinson's obsession with death and its pertinence to what appears to be a nervous breakdown in her late twenties. The symptoms, including her preoccupation with death, had become manifest years before she turned fifteen, when she wrote a friend about Mount Auburn cemetery in Boston; quoted a poet, Edward Young, on death; and noted that more than one hundred people had died recently in the city. Her letters are filled with inappropriate references to and questions about the last days of someone who had died. The culture of Puritanism and romanticism in her day dwelled upon death. And death from fatal diseases, rarely seen in the twenty-first century, was a daily occurrence in her small community. All these things contributed to her fixation on mortality, but the chief cause, writes Cody, was the mental disturbances in her youth.

Additional disturbances—less obviously ascribable to the transactions of Austin's love life and other external events—had for some years been rising to the surface of Emily Dickinson's thought and behavior from that hidden "fracture within" of whose existence she had been aware since childhood. . . .

John Cody, *After Great Pain: The Inner Life of Emily Dickinson.* Cambridge, MA: Harvard University Press, 1971. Copyright © 1971 by The President and Fellows of Harvard College. All rights reserved. Reproduced by permission of Harvard University Press. Incorporated excerpts from Emily Dickinson's letters from *The Letters of Emily Dickinson*, The Belknap Press of Harvard University Press. Copyright © 1958, 1986 The President and Fellows of Harvard College; 1914, 1924, 1932, 1942 by Martha Dickinson Bianchi; 1952 by Alfred Leete Hampson; 1960 by Mari L. Hampson. Reproduced by permission of the publishers and Trustees of Amherst College.

Dickinson's Mental Crisis

Though my purpose is to chart the increasing imbalance of Emily Dickinson's personality that led to her collapse in her late twenties, it is useful to refer to letters written long after the crisis to fill in the picture of the first symptoms. . . .

The following are the chief symptoms which first became manifest in the period of Emily Dickinson's life preceding her breakdown: depression, anxiety, estrangement, avoidance of gratification, extraction of pleasure from privation, preoccupation with death, withdrawal from social intercourse, agoraphobia [an anxiety disorder], fear of loss of emotional control, preternatural awareness of the mind's unconscious depths (symbolized by the "sea" images in her poems and letters), weakness of ego boundaries, and night fears. . . .

Preoccupation with Death

The sporadic depressions, anxieties, and estrangements that played a large part in Emily Dickinson's emotional life prior to her nervous breakdown are dwarfed by a symptom that manifested itself with inexorable persistence. This was her preoccupation with the theme of death.

As early as her fifteenth year, after she had been sent by her parents to Boston to recover her health and improve her spirits, she evinces an unusual intensity of interest in the subject in a letter to Abiah Root. She tells Abiah that since being in Boston she has "both seen & heard a great many wonderful things" and proceeds to list them, beginning: "I have been to Mount Auburn [cemetery]." A few passages later she quotes Edward Young's *Night Thoughts*: "Pay no moment but in just purchase of its worth & what it's worth, ask death beds. They can tell." After a few lines expressing her religious doubts and pleading with Abiah to visit her, the death theme appears again: "There have been many changes in Amherst since you was there. Many who were then in their bloom have gone to their last account & 'the mourners go about the streets.'" The body of the letter is followed by a long postscript in which a discussion of the warm weather leads again to the same theme: "There were over 100 deaths in Boston last week, a great many of them owing to the heat."

And recall the interesting intrusion of the death theme in an 1847 letter to Austin: "Did you think that it was my birth-day—yesterday?" Emily asks him; "I don't believe I am *17*. Is Jacob Holt [a dying neighbor] any better than when you wrote last & is there any hope of him?" For Emily each "happy birthday" was primarily just another milestone on the journey to the grave, as the sequence of associations here indicates.

A little over a year later, in a Valentine's Day letter to her cousin telling of the gaiety in Amherst, she observes that in another year "the present writers of these many missives [that is, the Valentines]" may be dead. The idea of death is intro-duced out of context by means of the flimsiest of transitional passages. What appears to be underscored here is her inner pressure to talk about the subject and her willingness to intro-duce it in the most inappropriate contexts.

Another inappropriate and strained introduction of her concern with death occurs in an 1850 letter to Jane Hum-phrey. Emily says: "Did you know that Payson had gone to Ohio to live? I was so sorry to have him go—but everyone is going—we shall all go—and not return again before long." Here, an ordinary change of residence of an acquaintance be-comes the springboard for her most obsessive theme.

Apparently Emily Dickinson's family were aware of her pe-culiar interest in mortality, though its significance as a symp-tom may not have been evident in her youth. Thus, Emily writes Austin: "Vinnie tells me *she* has detailed the *news*—she reserved the *deaths* for me."

Emily realized that she often brought up the subject of death inappropriately and acknowledged this propensity in an 1852 letter to Jane Humphrey. "I think of the grave very often," she writes, "and how much it has got of mine, and whether I can ever stop it from carrying off what I love; that makes me sometimes speak of it when I dont intend."

It has been advanced as a rational explanation of Emily Dickinson's fascination with the theme of death that her thoughts were naturally so directed because of the early demise of friends—that she was not particularly absorbed in the subject of death per se, but that she was concerned with the loss of specific individuals who had been or might be taken from her by death. In fact, she herself offers this explanation to T.W. Higginson: "Perhaps Death—gave me awe for friends—striking sharp and early, for I held them since—in a brittle love—of more alarm, than peace."

Threat of Mortality

However, if one examines her responses to the deaths of Sophia Holland and Leonard Humphrey, both of which were exceedingly intense reactions, it becomes clear that what afflicted her most profoundly was the fact of mortality itself and the precariousness of all life, including her own, rather than the concrete loss of a particular person. Though the death of Sophia Holland when Emily was thirteen precipitated a "fixed melancholy" which lasted for more than a month, the poet a few years later had forgotten the loss of her little chum; for when Leonard Humphrey died when Emily was nineteen, she wrote Abiah Root: "I never have laid my friends there [that is, in the grave], and forgot that they too must die; this is my first affliction." Similarly, three years after her tears for Humphrey had dried, she wrote to her brother after learning of B.F. Newton's death: "Oh, Austin, Newton is dead. The first of my own friends." Death itself always had a tremendous impact upon her. However, the dead themselves seem merely to have been the vehicles through which this obsession attained its grip on her imagination.

Throughout her life Emily Dickinson displayed an avid interest in death scenes. She thirsted for details; it was important to her to learn just how the dying felt in the face of imminent dissolution.

The first evidence in her correspondence of this eventually pressing need appears in a letter she wrote after the death of Newton to his minister, who was a complete stranger to her: "tell me if he was willing to die, and if you think him at Home, I should love so much to know certainly."

Inappropriate Curiosity About Death

In some obscure way death stimulated her. After Frazer Stearns was killed in battle she wrote the news to her Boston cousins. In its wealth of concrete details the letter indicates her eagerness in gathering and conveying the precise circumstances of death. "His big heart," she tells the cousins, "[was] shot away by a 'minie ball' . . . Just as he fell, in his soldier's cap, with his sword at his side, Frazier rode [as a corpse] through Amherst . . . He fell by the side of Professor Clark . . . lived ten minutes in a soldier's arms, asked twice for water—murmured just, 'My God!' and passed! Sanderson . . . made a box of boards in the night, put the brave boy in, covered with a blanket . . . They tell that Colonel Clark cried like a little child . . . Nobody here could look on Frazer. . . . The doctors would not allow it . . . you must come next summer, and we will mind ourselves of this young crusader."

Upon the death of a relative she asks the same cousins to return the favor: "you must tell us all you know about dear Myra's going." A note of—triumph?—seems to creep in to her questioning: "Was Myra willing to leave us all? I want so much to know if it was very hard, husband and babies and big life and sweet home by the sea [that is, all those prizes of life that Emily lacked]. I should think she would rather have stayed."

And after Dr. Holland's death Emily writes his widow: "I am yearning to know if he knew he was fleeing—if he spoke to you. Dare I ask if he suffered?"

After Charles Wadsworth died Emily wrote his friend J.D. Clark: "I hope you may tell me all you feel able of that last interview." Then, when Mr. Clark himself died, she directed her investigations to *his* death in a letter to his brother: "I am eager to know all you may tell me of those final Days." And again: "and though we cannot know the last, would you sometime tell me as near the last as your grieved voice is able?"

The same request is made of Helen H. Jackson's widower, a man Emily met only once: "[Will you] tell me a very little of her Life's close?" she inquires. And, at the same time, she writes Forrest Emerson: "Should she [a friend of Mrs. Jackson] know any circumstances of her life's close, would she perhaps lend it to you, that you might lend it to me?"

Her anxiety that her loved ones may be taken from her recurs again and again, and she frequently reminds her friends that life is transient. In an 1854 letter to Sue she asks, apropos of nothing, "Did you ever think, Susie, that there had been no grave here [meaning in her immediate family]?" And again to Sue: "And [if] you love me, come soon—this is *not* forever, you know, this mortal life of our's." And to the Hollands: "this world is short, and I wish, until I tremble, to touch the ones I love." And, at the close of an 1858 letter to Sue, death again appears as a non sequitur: "Good night . . . Since there are two varieties, we will say it softly—Since there are snowier beds, we'll talk a little every night, before we sleep in these!"

One of the clearest examples of the intrusive appearance of the death obsession without benefit of a justifying context occurs in an otherwise gay letter of thanks to Mrs. Haven sent upon receipt of some notes and a gift. Emily speaks of missing her friends and of her feelings upon passing the house where they formerly lived. "Your house has much of pathos," she says, "to those that pass who loved you . . . I shall miss the clustering frocks at the door, bye and bye when summer comes, unless myself in a *new* frock, am too far to see. How short, dear Mrs Haven!" The letter then concludes with this poem: "A darting fear—a pomp—a tear—/ A waking on a morn / to find that what one waked for, / inhales the different dawn."

The death theme owed its burgeoning to many springs. New England puritanism and nineteenth-century romanticism were both obsessed with death in their own particular way, and both, of course, impinged on Emily Dickinson incessantly from every quarter of her culture. It is important to realize also that the standard of public health in the twentieth century (in which communicable diseases are well controlled, dangerous epidemics are thought of as the exclusive property of undeveloped countries, early death is a rarity, and longevity is the rule) renders it difficult for us to appreciate the impact on our nineteenth-century ancestors of the omnipresence of death and the very real and constant menace it presented every day of their lives. *Emily Dickinson's Home*, by Millicent Todd Bingham, provides an impressive review of the many frequently fatal diseases, today all but unheard of, which were prevalent in nineteenth-century Amherst. . . .

The religious influences, the literary ones, and repeated actual confrontations with death undoubtedly made their contributions to Emily Dickinson's, preoccupation with mortality. But it should be apparent that these forces, in their convergence on the poet, found fertile psychological ground. Austin's letters to Susan exhibit no such preoccupation with death, and it is significant that Vinnie reserved the report of deaths for Emily. Moreover . . . the way she introduced the subject in her letters—abruptly and often irrelevantly—suggests that her conscious ruminations were stimulated as much by inner emotional disposition as by external impressions.

Death and Dying in
Emily Dickinson's Poetry

Death and Dickinson's Quickened Imagination

David Porter

David Porter, Professor Emeritus, Department of English, University of Massachusetts–Amherst, is the author of The Art of Emily Dickinson's Early Poetry *and* Emerson and Literary Change.

In the following viewpoint Porter says that Dickinson saw her life and art as so circumscribed by the physical world that she could not see a sphere that could provide her with ultimate answers, certitude, or a clear identity. The spiritual answers lay in death, at a time when diseases, childbirth, war, and accidents took the lives of many people. In a letter she said that the American Civil War had intensified the constant presence of death. Yet to the dying, she wrote, death was a novelty, a surprise that brought them truth for the first time. For Dickinson, although it brought anguish, death, as the final solution to life's mystery, called forth her imagination. It inspired her language, her symbolism. The idea of death had a formative effect on her style. It was behind her many metaphors, like that of the setting sun. Her poetic language became removed from the physical world and began to be increasingly focused on death, time, and immortality.

Without an active prejudice, no characterization of experience is possible, let alone a planned revolution. To face Dickinson's miscellaneousness, we ourselves seek the pattern of a bias marking her intelligence, her attention, her existence. But that enabling tendency does not exist. Her mind possessed no homing instrumentation. When she wrote to [Thomas Wentworth] Higginson in 1866 inviting him for the first time to visit her in Amherst, she located with incisive metaphoric language the truth of her condition. He had evidently asked about her interest in immortality. She replied: "You mention Immortality. That is the Flood subject." And then she made that keen self-estimate: "I was told that the Bank was the safest place for a Finless Mind." . . .

Death's Limitatation

I believe her word *circumference* meant to her the visible, natural periphery of all of God's realm to which the Bible's wisdom was the center. Yet at the center of her bold assertion lay only the vagueness of her self-identification. In two letters in the intensity of that summer of 1862 when she first sought from Higginson a definition of her power, she came figuratively, and of course cryptically, to that statement of purpose. "My Business is Circumference." She wrote then to [her friends] the Hollands: "*My* business is to love," "*My* business is to *sing*". Amid death and ignorance, her role was indefinite in a most intense way. . . .

Death Dictates Style

Decades of exegetical [critically explanatory] criticism, my own included, have projected Dickinson as a highly conscious, technically adept, sophisticated craftsman. The reading of her poetry benefited from this supposition because the intense linguistic activity in the poems became evident. Now our insights into her inordinate writing, conceptual vacuum, and canonical anarchy make possible new approaches to clusters of her problem poems. Broader understanding comes as we see more distinctly the problematics of Dickinson's artistic coherence and the emerging dissociation of her language from experience in the outer world. The first application of this knowledge can profitably be made to the significance of her preoccupation with death.

Yvor Winters . . . concluded that all of those poems that deal with experiences in the after-life—toward which the horses' heads were turned—are fraudulent. Yet so many of her poems address or assume that state implicitly that his characterization might extend to the largest proportion of the canon. What are we to do with the sunset poems, for example? They are not simply about sunsets, but about the promise of immortality in these vivid, emblematic endings. The vision of death or, to use her own somber metaphor, "the Drift of Eastern Gray," pervades her writing.

Dickinson's death poems in fact are more a matter of style than of idea. To put it concisely, death is the occasion for her language performance. . . .

Death as a Puzzle and as Novelty

But the subject of death held more for Dickinson than familiarity. It was simultaneously a matter of utter novelty. For this connoisseur of agitation it was also a matter of inherent movement. As novelty, it was "that odd Fork in Being's Road" and "a wild Night and a new Road." In a world of ceaseless surprise it was the essential surprise, "stupendous" as she said in a letter. "All other Surprise is at last monotonous, but the Death of the Loved is all moments—*now*". Her verse with her genius at lexical surprise solicited this phenomenon because it was needed. Her quick two-line movements gripped the change and novelty of death, took it as their occasion. In poem 1349, . . . she defined the quality of the subject that allowed the drama of her words: "in going is a Drama Staying cannot confer."

Death was also her figure of not knowing, a haunting presence to which as an artist she turned repeatedly. . . . It had an irresistible appeal for Dickinson because it was the "Sacred

Emily Dickinson's mentor, Thomas Wentworth Higginson, photographed in 1903. © Corbis.

Ignorance" in the Sunday school parables. It put an end to conjecture, the time when "subterfuge is done" and the temporary and the eternal "Apart—intrinsic—stand". Death was the single antidote to the great ignorance that was at the core of her problem of absent identity. "We do not think enough of the Dead as exhilarants," she wrote in a fragment, "they are not dissuaders but Lures—Keepers of that great Romance". . . .

Death and Identity

In its finality, death conferred identity, giving definition to a life as it "justified" Christ or outlined a season by its end. The lowliest acquire dignity in their moment of passing. All this was familiar the matic material for Dickinson, as here in this stanza of poem 1497:

> The hight of our portentous Neighbor
>
> We never know—
>
> Till summoned to his recognition
>
> By an Adieu—

In that movement into identity which she craved because of her own need, the dead have as she said "leaned into Perfectness". . . .

But beyond its significance to her as an emblem of completion, death meant most to her as an artist. It was the essential shock that called forth her ingenuity. She made her language grasp the absurdity of it, its "livid Surprise." That ingenuity . . . is the cause of the persistent novelty in reading Dickinson, death being the theme upon which she played the seemingly endless variations of which language is capable. . . . So often, it is the "enhancing Shadow" that enables her language of strangeness and her attempts to capture the fleeting moments that, like the seasons with their "fatal promptness," carried ever so subtly the strokes of fate. Out of that sacred ignorance of death and that generative poverty rose her ceaseless imagination. She came back and back again to play new words across its livid surprise, made the subject her principal trope, the source of her metaphors, and the emblem of her ignorance. Personified, death in her purview became some of the unique characters in our literature, including the country squire and the face of steel, a mid-nineteenth-century "Rock Drill." It was the first poverty out of which sprang her unique linguistic activity. . . .

She employed death in the way people use the weather as an excuse for communicating. She was not unconscious of her preoccupation and said as much in a letter to the Norcross cousins in the early 1860s, beginning her remark with a rare reference to death in the Civil War. She then turned to her own preoccupation:

> Sorrow seems more general than it did, and not the estate of a few persons, since the war began. . . .

Death and Language

If death, like memory, was for Dickinson a familiar realm linked always with language's preservative power, a place where parting is no more, where the loved ones that are lost reside, it was for the artist the emblem of absent knowledge that offered her the occasion not only to be epitaphic but also outrageous, witty, punning, self-dramatizing, and to display her independence. In a word, death was a summoner of style. If we attend to those death poems now with new eyes we can see the places where language as mimetic instrument or as rhetoric of consolation gives way in a characteristic Dickinson movement to an interplay of tropes. . . .

Death was the subject the culture held out for her, but it was her special emblem of the lack of identity she suffered. For this recluse exempt from experience it was, however trite in the literary conventions, a superb trigger to her style. To see this and to see as well how Dickinson's language has pulled away from actual experience, we have only to subtract from a Dickinson death poem the Sunday school conventions. What is left is her language, urgent and self-sufficient. The portion that is left is almost the whole shimmer of the poem.

Dickinson's Connection of Death to Time

Clark Griffith

Clark Griffith, whose work on Edgar Allan Poe and Emily Dickinson was groundbreaking, is a frequent subject of critical debate.

In the following excerpt Griffith says Dickinson contends that the passage of time brings on horrors, the chief of which is death. Her poems about time (like the course of a day) are really about her death mania, according to Griffith. She portrays the deaths of others, notably their corpses, as hideous mysteries that she is compelled to unravel. The poetic imaginings of her own death have an element of relief. So she sometimes viewed death, on one hand, as unbearably painful and fearful and, on the other, as something that she welcomed for herself. The death of her friends and family challenged her faith, at the same time that she saw it as a bringer of the final truth. The grieving survivors are stunned by death's chaos, which changes their universe. Dickinson fears time's alterations, especially its chief change, death. In poem 712 she writes of death in the first person as a wicked seducer who is abetted by a chaperone—immortality.

With time ... Miss Dickinson associates all that the human mind finds most deplorable. Foremost among time's horrors are death, toward which the temporal flow keeps hurrying the individual, and annihilation after death, a dismaying prospect which every action of time appears to confirm. . . .

Ambivalence Toward Death

But the light is quickly doused by darkness. In the first text, the sun rushes on to be enveloped in the "Western Mystery." The second candidly acknowledges that "how he set—I know not." As light symbolized life, so death is symbolically related to the loss of illumination. The "Western Mystery" is best understood as the eternal riddle of dying. The poet's failure to say how the sun set reflects her failure to see beyond life: her confusion about an action in Nature registers her inability to fathom death or to justify it philosophically.

With death, then, Emily Dickinson was almost uniquely preoccupied. Except perhaps for Melville, no writer of the American nineteenth century looked more habitually than she upon the skull beneath the skin, or was more visibly shaken by the spectacle. To a degree that is morbid and even ghoulish, Miss Dickinson's letters probe for answers among the recently bereaved. How did he die? she demands to know. Was he resigned? What was the look on his face? What were his last words? In the poetry, these same questions either reappear directly—

To know just how He suffered—would be dear

To know if any Human eyes were near . . .

To know if He was patient—part content—

Was dying as He thought—or different—

—or, at best, are transformed into great dramatic utterances. It seems fair to assert that the most gripping of Emily Dickinson's poems are poems centered around the questions of *what is death? why is death?* and *what is it like to die?*

Because the death poetry is so powerful and many-sided, we are justified, I think, in looking to it for more than a single reaction to the subject which it portrays. To say that Emily Dickinson lived in mortal dread of dying is, in a way, true

enough. Yet, like all such commonplaces, the statement re-
quires the most vigorous sort of qualification. It is when death
is presented as a spectacle—or when the corpse is laid out before her—that Miss Dickinson's speaker is most openly ap-
palled. Then she beholds death as a moral and physical ugliness; baffled by this deformity, she recoils in terror from the
sheer complexity of the issues involved. When, by contrast,
she thinks of death as a fact about herself—when she sees it
as a condition into which she is entering, rather than as the
condition of someone else—the speaker's response is likely to
be very different. If her terror is still there, it now becomes a
terror that is underlain by a strange sense of relief. Almost,
she comes to welcome death, to look with perfect equanimity
upon the fact of dissolution, to conceive of personal annihilation as a state to be desired.

The result is that within the large body of death poetry,
two totally opposed viewpoints often appear side by side. The
same set of topics that can give rise to frustration and tension
will likewise sometimes serve as the bases for hope and release. Ultimately, I believe, we shall discover that the thought
of dying could soothe as well as lacerate Emily Dickinson—
and that the certainty of her own death was at once the supreme problem she had to face, but also a kind of psychological outlet, without which her life would have been quite
unendurable.

Interpreting the Deaths of Others

In the grimmest and least equivocal of her poems about dying, Emily Dickinson's speakers function as bereaved onlook-
ers who recount the circumstances of someone else's passing.
As in the following example, the poet and other mourners follow a loved one to the brink of death; then, left themselves
among the living, they seek, without much success, to inter-
pret the experience they have watched:

Emily Dickinson's gravestone (in Amherst, Massachusetts) bears the epitaph "CALLED BACK," which was the entire text of the last letter she wrote to her cousins in May 1886. It refers to the title of an 1883 novella by Hugh Conway. © AP Images/Beth Harpaz.

The last Night that She lived

It was a Common Night

Except the Dying—that to Us

Made Nature different

We noticed smallest things—

Things overlooked before

By this great light upon our Minds

Italicized—as 'twere.

As We went out and in

Between Her final Room

And Rooms where Those to be alive

Tomorrow were, a Blame

That others should exist

While She must finish quite

A Jealousy for Her arose

So nearly infinite—

We waited while She passed—

It was a narrow time—

Too jostled were Our Souls to speak

At length the notice came.

She mentioned and forgot—

Then lightly as a Reed

Bent to the Water, struggled scarce—

Consented, and was dead—

And We—We placed the Hair—

And drew the Head erect—

And then an awful leisure was

Our faith to regulate—

Clearly, the emphasis in the poem lies with the living. The point of view is specifically theirs, so that dying and death are treated throughout as events which the living perceive. At the end, it is the living who must continue to act; when the anonymous *She* has become a corpse, the mourners are still faced with the terrible task of looking for consolation or purpose in the scene before them. These facts shape the theme of the poem, making it less a study of death as such than one of grief and of a crisis in faith. They likewise help to account for the seemingly deliberate ugliness out of which the poem has been wrought. . . .

Death and Faith

Emily Dickinson's method is shaped by, and it remains beautifully compatible with, her meaning. To be confronted by a corpse is the crudest, the ugliest, and the most harrowing experience that she can imagine. For one thing, the confrontation exacts from the living their last, pitiful homage to the dead. Whatever their feelings, the living must continue to act; in a kind of stunned agony, they set about placing the hair and drawing the head erect. But, what is far more painful, the living find that the perception of death results in a violent derangement of their own faith. Drawn up before a corpse—brought into the presence of the frozen features and the unbroken silence of the dead—the living glimpse the one philosophical problem which no amount of hope can palliate. They exist in a moment of intense mystery—in the *narrow time*, when every energy is focussed upon solving the unsolveable. All they can see ahead of them is a perpetuation of the mystery. Death has shattered belief; after death, there can come only tomorrow's *awful leisure*, when the ruins of faith will have to be picked up and, if possible, regulated anew. . . .

The first response involves the trial of faith. . . . Contemplating the dead, the living are deserted by any sense they might once have had of an orderly universe. Their souls become *jostled*—that is, crowded by thoughts which question the fitness of things. As, literally, the mourners tread from room to room in the bereaved house, so, symbolically, they are walking to and fro through a maze of doubts and uncertainties. Eventually, a kind of envy of the dead springs up:

> That others should exist
>
> While She must finish quite
>
> A Jealousy for Her arose
>
> So nearly infinite—

At least, in death, the corpse knows—knows whether death leads to anything beyond itself. For the survivors, there is nothing to be seen except a long future of pondering this issue—and of realizing that, so long as one is alive, no real answer is ever likely to be forthcoming. . . .

Death as Transformation

In Emily Dickinson's terms, then, the result of death is a complete transformation of being. That which was like ourselves, sharing our physical structure, our responses, our mode of behavior, is suddenly and utterly altered. The poet's own reaction is centered around the fact of the alteration. . . .

She makes bereavement vivid and concrete by dramatizing it as

The Sweeping up the Heart

And putting Love away

We shall not want to use again

Until Eternity.

The significance of these household tropes is two-fold. First of all, they reinforce a point made earlier, reminding us again of how in the presence of death, which is chaos, Emily Dickinson's survivors seek to reorder their lives through some tightly disciplined movement, some bare and yet ceremonious act. . . . Like the perception of time, the perception of the dead is for Emily Dickinson a source of unremitting horror. She must ponder death through completely mature eyes for the simple reason that there is no pretense which can minimize the terrors of the corpse—and no averting of the eyes which will blind one to the dilemmas and uncertainties that the existence of the corpse elicits.

So, viewed in the form of an *objective* condition, death can only unsettle the viewer, arousing her to a sense of loss and grief, or to feelings of absolute futility. . . .

At the Point of Death

Miss Dickinson's intentions in the second category of her death poems may be readily described. She attempts an imaginative construction of her own death: tries, in effect, to catch herself at the very center of the act of dying. As in the time-and-change texts, consequently, the writing stresses a momentous transition; now, however, the transition takes place from within, so that it bridges the period when life starts to drain away to the exact moment when death arrives and the world around her has receded from the speaker. At her most brilliant, Emily Dickinson forges these matters into a poetry that is without parallel in the English language.

One supposes that her most famous, if not necessarily her best, example is "The Chariot":

> Because I could not stop for Death—
>
> He kindly stopped for me—
>
> The carriage held but just ourselves
>
> And Immortality.
>
> We slowly drove—He knew no haste
>
> And I had put away
>
> My labor and my leisure too,
>
> For His Civility—
>
> We passed the School, where Children strove
>
> At Recess—in the Ring—
>
> We passed the fields of Gazing Grain—
>
> We passed the Setting Sun—
>
> Or rather—He passed Us—
>
> The Dews drew quivering and chill—
>
> For only Gossamer, my Gown—
>
> My Tippet—only Tulle—
>
> We paused before a House that seemed
>
> A swelling of the Ground—

The Roof was scarcely visible—

The Cornice—in the Ground—

Since then—'tis Centuries—and yet

Feels shorter than the Day

I first surmised the Horses Heads

Were toward Eternity—

Death as Seducer

For "The Chariot" does rest upon a narrative basis—that is, involves characters, an episode, a plot-line of sorts—and the narrative, in turn, has certain conventional literary associations. Up to the door, there come riding not one but two callers: observe that the carriage is occupied by both Death *and* Immortality. Presumably they dally for a little, then presently they ride off with the Lady-Poet into the sunset. . . . Words like *kindness* and *civility* can . . . , be accepted at face value. They mean that Death comes as a gentleman, motivated by honorable intentions, and concerned only with carrying the Lady to her bridal rooms in Heaven. . . . Death-as-lover affixes the part played by Immortality. This silent partner on the drive must be visualized as nothing less than a chaperone. Saying nothing, but always sternly ensconced on a rear seat, Immortality sanctifies the relationship between Death and Lady, keeps the relationship beyond reproach, ensures that the journey into darkness will have a respectable ending. Immortality's function, when we stop to think about it, could hardly be more proper, therefore—or more strictly orthodox.

But in the [sentimental] novel[s popular in the late eighteenth and early nineteenth centuries], "courtly love" was not always this innocent a pastime. . . . It was sometimes the cunning seducer who came calling, and who whisked the Lady away quite against her will. If Emily Dickinson's personification is seen in this guise, a re-evaluation of the whole drama becomes necessary. Death is no longer to be thought of as a kindness; he is someone depraved and malevolent. In the slow, deliberate pacing of his journey, we perhaps glimpse the arrogance of Death, his bland disrespect for human wishes. Certainly the flimsiness of the Lady's apparel—

> For only Gossamer, my Gown—
>
> My Tippet—only Tulle—

—can only recall us to how vulnerable humankind is when Death attacks. But the greatest change is reserved for Immortality, who, in the second reading of "The Chariot," abruptly ceases to chaperone, and becomes, instead, party to a wicked fraud. As Death now violates, so Immortality now betrays. Both have used the demeanor of courtliness in order to deceive; the victim of both is the helpless human being.

Our reaction to the total poem will hinge ultimately upon how we have interpreted these narrative details. Regardless of which version seems preferable, the journey itself deserves detailed analysis. As the expedition proceeds, the Lady-Poet is leaving life; it disappears behind her like a receding landscape. . . .

But what, aside from the grave, is the destination of the chariot? Are the horses pointed beyond anything more than the house in the ground? Emily Dickinson specifically declines to say. The word with which she ends the text is *Eternity*—in this context a strikingly ambiguous word, one that can grow meaningful only in the light of our response to the narrative situation. Provided we saw Death as the gallant lover and Immortality as a protector, we will presume that dying represented a benefit, and that the Lady-Poet was borne by her escorts to an Eternity of immortal life. Provided we saw Death as seducer and Immortality as his partner in crime, however, we must infer a vastly different outcome, supposing that the Lady was raped of life, and afterward abandoned to the earth and to the void of Eternal nothingness. . . .

Death Is Both Desire and Despair

Almost every day, as Conrad Aiken once said of her, Emily Dickinson must consciously have died a little. And almost every year since the discovery of her poetry, a critic has announced that death was the one subject which could drive Emily Dickinson to an absolutely limitless despair. What, then, shall we make of this fact: that the more personal death becomes in the poetry, the more the poet's despair is qualified— the more her response is divided between despair and desire?

In one way, [Sigmund] Freud's analysis of the psychology of death may help. The whole informing principle of a "death wish" involves contradictory impulses that are remarkably similar to Emily Dickinson's. Excessive brooding over death is assumed to reflect one's morbid aversion to the thought of dying; but it also bespeaks the morbid attraction that one feels for the very prospect which has been rejected. Certainly Miss Dickinson would appear to possess, in rare abundance, each classic symptom of the death wish—not only the tendency to brood about death, but likewise the simultaneous fear-and-fascination which prompts the brooding, and in which, again and again, the brooding must always culminate. . . .

Clearly, the fear of time shaped her more despairing conception of death. Change in all forms repelled her; hence death, the ultimate in change, had to strike her as an especially abhorrent prospect. Moreover, she saw time as divesting all worldly events of order and stability. Accordingly, time could only confirm her suspicion that the end of life was to be one further incoherence.

Representation and Personification of Death in Dickinson's Poetry

Thomas H. Johnson

Thomas H. Johnson was a professor at the Lawrenceville School and edited The Complete Poems of Emily Dickinson, *without which, it is agreed, Dickinson would not have achieved the recognition she has today.*

Dickinson's poems about death focus on a variety of subjects, including the corpse itself and the transition from life to death, notes Johnson in this excerpt. They take the form of personification, elegies, and epitaphs. But common to all these approaches is the cessation of communication with the dead. In showing the dying person searching for death's mysteries, she reveals her longing to know those secrets. In "I heard a Fly buzz—when I died," the reader sees the very moment of death made commonplace by the lowly fly. Sometimes Dickinson makes death a character, often a tyrant. He is also a suitor, promising gifts, and sometimes a monster to be hunted down in his "den." In "Because I could not stop for Death," Johnson sees the dying speaker as facing the end of time and motion. Death itself is a kindly gentleman, according to Johnson. He is her escort who fades into the background at journey's end.

Other poets of comparable stature have made the theme of death central in much of their writing. Emily Dickinson did so in hers to an unusual degree. In one way or another

Thomas H. Johnson, *Emily Dickinson: An Interpretive Biography*. Cambridge, MA: The Belknap Press, 1955. Copyright © 1955 by The President and Fellows of Harvard College. Copyright © renewed 1983 by Thomas Herbert Johnson. All rights reserved. Reproduced by permission of Harvard University Press. Incorporated Emily Dickinson poems from *The Poems of Emily Dickinson*, The Belknap Press of Harvard University Press. Copyright © 1951, 1955, 1979, 1983 by The President and Fellows of Harvard College. Reprinted by permission of the publishers and the Trustees of Amherst College.

she has drawn it into the texture of some five or six hundred poems. "All but Death," she wrote in 1863, "can be adjusted," and concludes:

Death—unto itself exception—

Is exempt from Change.

Much later in life she came to feel that "Maturity only enhances mystery, never decreases it." She viewed death from every possible angle, and left a record of her emotions and of her ideas about it in her poems. Death is a terror to be feared and shunned. It is a hideous, inequitable mistake; a trick played on trusting humanity by a sportive, insensate deity. It is a welcome relief from mortal ills. It is the blessed means to eternal happiness. But which of the attitudes is most valid, what assumptions about it are really true, she never decided.

Variety of Approaches to Death

The poems on death fall into three groups. There are those which are concerned with the physical demise of the body some describing the act of dying with clinical detachment, some with emotional vehemence. Others muse upon death or depict the face and form of the body on which the gazer's attention is riveted. There are the poems in which death, the suitor, is personified—in which the theme deals less with life here and now, or of life to come, than with the precise moment of transition from one state to the other. And there are also the elegies and epitaphs—lyrical commemorations of friends or of personages whom she has admired, like Elizabeth Barrett Browning or Charlotte Brontë.

There seems to he one persistent thought that binds together this very large number of poems on death. It is the knowledge that death snaps the lines of communication with those we have known and loved, and creates the uncertainty in the minds of all mortals whether that communication can ever be reëstablished. She gave expression thus in 1864 to the basic human wonderment:

Those who have been in the Grave the long-
est—

Those who begin Today—

Equally perish from our Practise—

Death is the further way—

Foot of the Bold did least attempt it—

It—is the White Exploit—

Once to achieve, annuls the power

Once to communicate—

Death, whether occurring in the recesses of the past or in this instant of time, succeeds in accomplishing the one thing about which she felt a gathering terror. Each such event left her irrecoverably out of touch with those she had loved. "A Coffin—is a small Domain," she says in the same year,

Yet able to contain

A Rudiment of Paradise

In it's diminished Plane.

A Grave—is a restricted Breadth—

Yet ampler than the Sun—

And all the Seas He populates

And Lands He looks upon

To Him who on it's small Repose

Bestows a single Friend—

Circumference without Relief—

Or Estimate—or End—

Such a terror can express itself in a variety of ways, and her poems were not only the means by which she relieved her apprehensions, but the medium through which she adjusted herself to the necessity and to the pleasure of living and being richly alive. . . .

Searching for Connections at the Moment of Death

"How many times these low feet staggered" is written from the point of view of one who stands alone in a room gazing at a dead body. Intimate touches associate the deceased with her homely labors. One cannot move the "adamantine fingers" which will never again wear a thimble. Dull flies buzz, the sun shines bravely through the "freckled pane," and a cobweb now swings "fearless" from the ceiling. In "I've seen a Dying Eye," she describes the search of the dying one for something just before the sight is obscured by death:

> Then Cloudier become—
>
> And then—obscure with Fog—
>
> And then—he soldered down
>
> Without disclosing what it be
>
> 'Twere blessed to have seen—

The search, it is clear, is in fact being made by the poet who, in the presence of death, hopes to find an answer to the riddle of death. It belongs to the same order of poems as "'Tis so appalling it exhilirates," in which she concludes that

> Looking at Death, is Dying—
>
> Just let go the Breath—
>
> And not the pillow at your Cheek
>
> So Slumbereth—
>
> Others, Can wrestle—
>
> Your's, is done—
>
> And so of Wo, bleak dreaded—come,
>
> It sets the Fright at liberty—

And Terror's free—

Gay, Ghastly, Holiday! . . .

Imaging the Moment of Death

Remarkable for its virtuosity, "I heard a Fly buzz—when I died," belongs to a somewhat different order among the lyrics which ponder the crises of sorrow. It appears to have been written in 1862. With that combination of condensed precision and eloquence which give her best poems their rank, she transmits the sensations which she imagines she might feel during the last moments before death. The bereaved family at the bedside are past the point of tears, for the moment of death has arrived.

And Breaths were gathering firm

For that last Onset—when the King

Be witness—in the Room—

A stillness such as that "between the heaves of storm" prepares the reader physically to hear the final agonizing gasp of the dying. The buzzing fly, so familiar a part of the natural order of persistent household discomforts, is brought in at the last to give the touch of petty irritabilities that are concomitant with living—and indeed—with dying.

With Blue—uncertain stumbling Buzz—

Between the light—and me—

And then the Windows failed—and then

I could not—see to see—

It is of course because Emily Dickinson had from childhood felt an unusual sensitivity about such events that she is here uniquely able to give reality to the moment. . . .

Personifying Death

A quite different order of poems are those which personify Death, a nebulous creature at first, who soon develops the stature of a true character of fiction. "One dignity delays for

all," written in 1859, pictures Death as a potentate, almost ori-
ental in the absoluteness of his sway and the splendor of his
court. His colors are purple, and thus doubly associated: with
royalty and with the color of the ample bow of ribbons at-
tached at the time of death to the front door of New England
houses. The "dignity" which none can avoid includes, besides
the purple, a coach, footmen, a chamber, and a state gathering. There will be bells too for the processional march, with
solemn service and a hundred raised hats. This pomp, sur-
passing ermine, death prepares:

> When simple you, and I,
>
> Present our meek escutcheon
>
> And claim the rank to die!

Exactly the same ceremony of investiture is described in the
slightly later poem "Wait till the majesty of Death/ Invests so
mean a brow," where "this democrat," dressed in "everlasting
robes," receives the homage of "obsequious angels." Twice
again (in 1862) he is the despot. Here too as earlier in "I
heard a Fly buzz when I died," we wait "For that last Onset—
when the King/ Be witnessed—in the Room." But in "Triumph may be of several kinds" Death, that "Old Imperator,"
has been met and vanquished by his adversary Faith. This is
the last poem in which Emily Dickinson imagines death as a
swollen tyrant. She now returns the morality puppet to its box
because she already has created one of the most extraordinary
characters in American literature. . . .

In "The only Ghost I ever saw" the personification is likewise both concrete and abstract. Death is a person and also a
force of nature. He wears a lacy garment and moves with silent, rapid gait. Shy in her presence, he politely engages her in
a "transcient" interview. Recalling his elusiveness and the
sound of his diminishing laughter, she is in the mood to say:
"And God forbid I look behind/ Since that Appalling Day."

It is the well-bred gentility of Death, who takes on the nature of a cavalier suitor, that distinguishes him in several poems written in 1862. He woos with gifts in "For Death—or rather," offering "Room, Escape from Circumstances, and a Name." But the entreated one remains perplexed, not knowing how to compare Death's gifts with Life's, since the equivalent of Life's values cannot be known until we die. . . .

In "Death is a subtle suitor," written some twelve years later, Death still woos stealthily by "pallid innuendoes and dim approach"; and he carries his intended bride to a troth and to unknown kindred who are as "responsive as porcelain." On some occasions he is a genteel householder whose rooms are made habitable by pale furniture and metallic peace. Sometimes he holds debate with the spirit. "Death is a Dialogue between/ The Spirit and the Dust," she says, in which the spirit, not deigning to pursue the argument, turns away after laying off for evidence of the encounter "An Overcoat of Clay." He is also a despoiler, a Grendel [monster from the epic poem *Beowulf*] to be hunted to his ravine or chased to his den.

The Frost of Death was on the Pane—

"Secure your Flower" said he.

Like Sailors fighting with a Leak

We fought Mortality.

Our passive Flower we held to Sea—

To Mountain—To the Sun—

Yet even on his Scarlet Shelf

To crawl the Frost begun—

We pried him back

Ourselves we wedged

Himself and her between,

Yet easy as a narrow Snake

He forked his way along

Till all her helpless beauty bent

And then our wrath begun—

We hunted him to his Ravine

We chased him to his Den—

We hated Death and hated Life

And nowhere was to go—

Than Sea and continent there is

A larger—it is Woe . . .

Death as the Greatest Character in Literature

In 1863 Death came into full stature as a person. "Because I could not stop for Death" is a superlative achievement wherein Death becomes one of the great characters of literature.

It is almost impossible in any critique to define exactly the kind of reality which her character Death attains, simply because the protean shifts of form are intended to forestall definition. A poem can convey the nuances of exultation, agony, compassion, or any mystical mood. But no one can successfully define mysticism because the logic of language has no place for it. One must therefore assume that the reality of Death, as Emily Dickinson conceived him, is to be perceived by the reader in the poems themselves. Any analysis can do no more than suggest what may be looked for.

In "Because I could not stop for Death" Emily Dickinson envisions Death as a person she knew and trusted, or believed that she could trust. He might be any Amherst gentleman, . . . or any of the coming lawyers or teachers or ministers whom she remembered from her youth, with whom she had exchanged valentines, and who at one time or another had acted as her squire.

Because I could not stop for Death—

He kindly stopped for me—

The Carriage held but just Ourselves—

And Immortality.

The carriage holds but the two of them, yet the ride, as she states with quiet emphasis, is a last ride together. Clearly there has been no deception on his part. They drive in a leisurely manner, and she feels completely at ease. Since she understands it to be a last ride, she of course expects it to be unhurried. Indeed, his graciousness in taking time to stop for her at that point and on that day in her life when she was so busy she could not possibly have taken time to stop for him, is a mark of special politeness. She is therefore quite willing to put aside her work. And again, since it is to be her last ride, she can dispense with her spare moments as well as her active ones.

We slowly drove—He knew no haste

And I had put away

My labor and my leisure too

For His Civility—

She notes the daily routine of the life she is passing from. Children playing games during a school recess catch her eye at the last. And now the sense of motion is quickened. Or perhaps more exactly one should say that the sense of time comes to an end as they pass the cycles of the day and the seasons of the year, at a period of both ripeness and decline.

We passed the School, where Children strove

At Recess—in the Ring—

We passed the Fields of Gazing Grain—

We passed the Setting Sun—

How insistently "passed" echoes through the stanza! She now conveys her feeling of being outside time and change, for she corrects herself to say that the sun passed them, as it of course does all who are in the grave. She is aware of dampness and cold, and becomes suddenly conscious of the sheerness of the dress and scarf which she now discovers that she wears.

> Or rather—He passed Us—
>
> The Dews drew quivering and chill
>
> For only Gossamer, my Gown—
>
> My Tippet—only Tulle—

The two concluding stanzas, with progressively decreasing concreteness, hasten the final identification of her "House." It is the slightly rounded surface "of the Ground," with a scarcely visible roof and a cornice "in the Ground." To time and seasonal change, which have already ceased, is now added motion. Cessation of all activity and creativeness is absolute. At the end, in a final instantaneous flash of memory, she recalls the last objects before her eyes during the journey: the heads of the horses that bore her, as she had surmised they were doing from the beginning, toward—it is the last word—"Eternity."

> We paused before a House that seemed
>
> A Swelling of the Ground—
>
> The Roof was scarcely visible—
>
> The Cornice—in the Ground—
>
> Since then—'tis Centuries—and yet
>
> Feels shorter than the Day
>
> I first surmised the Horses Heads
>
> Were toward Eternity—

Gradually, too, one realizes that Death as a person has receded into the background, mentioned last only impersonally in the opening words "We paused" of the fifth stanza, where his services as squire and companion are over. In this poem concrete realism melds into "awe and circumference" with matchless economy.

Dickinson Affirms Vitality in Life and Death

Robert Weisbuch

Robert Weisbuch, who has written books and articles on nineteenth-century American literature, was a professor and an administrator at the University of Michigan before becoming president of Drew University.

Typology is a system of comparisons between two entities. Types are foreshadowers, and antitypes are the fulfillment of what has been foreshadowed. Using these devices, Weisbuch says, Emily Dickinson brings up the euphemisms her society used in talking about death. The euphemism for "death" in Dickinson's world was "gone away," a phrase often used to inform children of the death of someone: the person had not died but had gone away. Dickinson also tended to deny death by, for example, belittling the god who caused deaths. The dying person's mementos create a type, foreshadowing our own death. In several poems death is represented by all things negative—for example, the fly. In others Dickinson sees death as opening up a larger world without end, giving us greater consciousness, which brings greater pain for both mourners and the mourned. Still Weisbuch argues that Dickinson retained her belief in an afterlife.

Dickinson . . . "started Early" on her contemplative journey toward death. At age twenty-one she tells her friend Jane Humphrey, "I think of the grave very often, and how much it has got of mine, and whether I can ever stop it from carrying off what I love; that makes me sometimes speak of it when I dont intend" (L 86). . . .

I am saying that nearly every poem Dickinson wrote has to do with death, with endings. Is all this analogy-making thus a charade, a mask to disguise a grotesque obsession? To the contrary, death has a special . . . status which necessitates analogy. Death is what we know least through direct experience. It is the "spacious arm . . . / That none can understand" (1625) and, more terrifyingly, "the Riddle" through which each of us must "walk" (50). Endings in nature are similarly confounding. "I'll tell you how the Sun rose—" one poem begins confidently, "But how he set—I know not—." . . .

In a sense, death and its aftermath is not a theme at all, not so much a theme with assignable topics of rational discourse (this statement's assertion of resurrection will be questioned or denied in many poems) as a raw material for speculations, even for speculations about the limits of speculation. . . .

Focus on the Mourner

In a quasi-chronological manner, we are going to follow the course of a Dickinsonian death. At each stage of the death, we shall consider the emotions in Dickinsonian experience which foreshadow the antitype. While earlier we concerned ourselves with how Dickinson makes connections, now we will be concerned with what she connects and why.

We begin the narrative with the persona in black, standing at the grave to mourn the death of a loved one. Though Dickinson's truncated elegies do not often include such elegiac conventions as the invocation to the muse, the critique of the clergy, or the sympathetic lament of nature, they do continue one great elegiac tradition: the focus of interest is on the mourner rather than on the mourned. In fact, Dickinson usually does not name, even by conventional epithets, the particular friend who has died.

The euphemism for "died" is "gone away"; Dickinson's type for the death of a friend is the geographical separation of friends in life. In itself, the equation of separation and death is hardly surprising. The fear that a loved one with whom we cannot communicate is in dire straits is a commonplace irrationality. The Civil War, which took place during Dickinson's most prolific years of creation, could only exaggerate the fear that "going away" was a preparation for death, since many Amherst friends did "go away" and then "were gone" forever. But Dickinson's equation of separation and death, of missing and mourning, begins much earlier, at age twenty in a letter to her close friend Jane Humphrey: "When I knew Vinnie [Lavinia, Emily's sister, who was away at school] must go I clung to you as the dearer than ever friend—but when the grave opened—and swallowed you both—I murmured—and thought I had a right to—I hav'nt changed my mind yet—either" (L 30). Dickinson here insists that, for all practical purpose, leave-taking *is* death; at least, it appears so to the one left behind, desolate. "I would have you here, all here," Dickinson tells another youthful friend, Abiah Root, "where I can *see* you, and *hear* you." . . .

In a self-criticism typical of her skeptical world, she will criticize the figure of separation as absolutely insufficient. For instance, the comfort given a child by the euphemism "gone away" itself gives way to fear and awe as the journey is reinterpreted:

I noticed People disappeared

When but a little child—

Supposed they visited remote

Or settled Regions wild—

Now know I—They both visited

And settled Regions wild.

But did because they died

A Fact withheld the little child—

(1149)

The substitution of the fact "died" for the surmised "disappeared" changes the sense of the journey so completely that Dickinson has only to repeat the exact words which describe a pioneer adventure to describe a vision of Eternity. Here the antitype is the grown-up version of the child's type, but elsewhere innocence may be retrieved in maturity as a rationalization to deny the "Fact":

We'll pass without the parting

So to spare

Certificate of Absence—

Deeming where

I left Her I could find Her

If I tried—

This way, I keep from missing

Those that died.

(996)

The willfully delusive speaker not only wishes to deny the antitype; she wants to pretend that the absence is on her part, that she has put away her friend like a discarded doll which can be found and picked up once more. This refusal to write an elegy, to acknowledge the special nature of this absence, is so self-consciously transparent that it only emphasizes the ab-

solute finality it pretends to deny. . . . It is the emotional difficulty of admitting the difference between separation and
death, missing and mourning, that Dickinson here dramatizes.

Occasionally, in order to negate that emotional difficulty,
Dickinson will evolve a traditional Christian consolation.
Since the absent return in life, these poems reason, why not
those who are absent because of death? To her absent brother
Austin, Dickinson writes, "none of us are gone where we cannot come home again, and the separations *here* are but for a
little while" (L 104). The death-separation, she implies, is only
longer. By extension, since the dead are only somewhere else,
why will I not rejoin them when I die? Dickinson thus projects
a heaven of restored personal relations. "Fleshless Lovers"
meet for a "second time" before "the Judgment Seat of God"
and, this time, they wed (625). Unfortunately, when such a
poem asks, "Was Bridal—e'er like This?" we are all too tempted
to answer in the negative. Likewise, in "There Came a Day at
Summer's full," a single day of love, a summer day so "full"
that it is described as a form of immortality in time, ends in a
separation whose finality is denied:

And so when all the time had leaked,

Without external sound,

Each bound the Other's Crucifix—

We gave no other Bond—

Sufficient troth, that we shall rise

Deposed—at length, the Grave—

To that new Marriage,

Justified—through Calvaries of Loves—

(322)

There is nothing inherently wrong with this fiction. . . .

In 1861, rioting secessionists fire upon the Sixth Massachusetts Infantry Regiment in Baltimore, Maryland, during the American Civil War. Also that year, Emily Dickinson's friend Frazer Stearns was killed in Annapolis, Maryland. © Corbis.

Death and Religion

This too-easy denial of death's terrifying finality can create powerful poems when it is not allowed to become a flat-footed article of faith. It can become a proud and fierce assertion of human over supernatural values:

God is indeed a jealous God—

He cannot bear to see

That we had rather not with Him

But with each other play.

(1719)

God as a lonesome Nobodaddy kills us for company, and Dickinson's revenge is to create a supernatural fiction in which we continue to play with each other. . . .

The Dying Remind Us of Our Own Mortality

It is the middlemost moment in her narrative of doom, the very act of dying, that most fires Dickinson's imagination. From that moment evolve two great and troubled masterpieces: "I heard a Fly buzz—when I died" and "I felt a Funeral, in my Brain." To get at these crucial poems, we must consider a group of lesser, but fully remarkable, poems which form a bridge between the elegiac analogy of separation and death and the analogy which informs the two masterpieces, an analogy between psychological pain and one's own death.

These are "Hamlet" poems, in which the mourner typologically leaps into the grave. That is, the mourner, by a psychological metaphor, imitates the death of the loved one; and, like him, the mourner achieves a completed understanding through an intensity of pain. We die only once, but before that we project ourselves into death many times, whenever another "leaves" or dies: "Parting is one of the exactions of a Mortal Life," Dickinson writes to Mrs. Holland. "It is bleak—like Dying, but occurs more times" (L 399). The distance between the type of separation and the antitype of death—now, one's own death—is closed.

There is nothing luxuriously altruistic in this extreme empathy; it is based on the fact of mortality, the fact that the mourner, too, will die. Thus in one poem Dickinson has us peer into an "Ebon Box" filled with mementos of the dead—withered flowers, yellow letters, antique trinkets, a curl. Symbols of dead nature, dead youth, dead affections, and human death itself are contained in that box, and yet we shut it again, "As if the little Ebon Box /Were none of our affair!" (169). As if . . . and yet that box both contains our past and foreshadows our fate, when we too will be placed in a larger ebon box. . . .

The dead are both cold and transcendent, under the ground and beyond the sky. The imitative mourner undergoes a similarly mixed fate. His woe paralyzes and enlarges him. In "A Coffin—is a small Domain," Dickinson plays not only on this compound of loss and gain but also on the likeness of the mourner and the mourned:

A Grave—is a restricted Breadth—

Yet ampler than the Sun—

And all the Seas He populates

And Lands He looks upon

To Him who on its small Repose—

Bestows a single Friend—

Circumference without Relief—

Or Estimate—or End—

(943)

Dickinson's syntactical shock-tactic here is to set up the earlier stanza as though it refers to the body in the coffin and then to disclose in the final stanza that she is describing instead (or in addition) the condition of the mourner who places the friend on the coffin-bed. The coffin's narrow space nonetheless contains the largest possibility, an immortality which dwarfs nature. Just so, thoughts of the coffin on the mourner's part give him the largest range of speculation—too large, "without Relief," to be suitably comforting. Even the enlargement, of consciousness may be more torturous than benevolent. . . .

Death as Both Loss and Gain

Dickinson's two finest poems of dying emphasize different aspects of pain and power along with a double sense of loss and gain. In "I heard a Fly buzz—when I died," . . . there is no ostensible suggestion that the poem is describing anything "earlier" than how the mind feels when it dies. Yet the scene of this "last onset" is so exclusively the mind that it cannot help suggesting figural, experiential states of consciousness. . . .

The voice begins by attempting to define the peculiarity of its moment:

I heard a Fly buzz—when I died—

The Stillness in the Roon

Was like the Stillness in the Air—

Between the Heaves of Storm—

(465)

We know nothing about the fly's buzz yet except that its sound stands out against a background of silence. . . .

The mourners are consoled and rewarded, the dying one is prepared to die. But as everyone waits for the king, "There interposed a Fly—"

With Blue—uncertain stumbling Buzz—

Between the light—and me—

And then the Windows failed—and then

I could not see to see—

(465)

The functions of the fly are various. . . . First, the fly is a dramatic disappointment. We expected a king, and so the passage from the world becomes pathetic in a macabre way. However royal one may yet become through death, its onset is purely physical and negative. (The world will end not with a bang but with a buzz.) In addition, though the fly seems to bring or at least focus death, its buzzing flight represents natural vitality and thus emphasizes the persona's paralysis. Finally, this fly is a past and future annoyance. Dickinson does not like flies in her life, and when she wishes to suggest doubt about an afterlife, insects often come to mind. . . .

[The] minimal, hard-won belief, often interrupted by doubt but always reasserting itself, that vitality continues, transformed, after death, and in life increases through awe and pain, is sufficient. It is sufficient to keep Dickinson on the path of discovery, even when that path leads beyond the known and the mind transgresses the bounds of safety. It is this willingness to persevere in danger which earns Dickinson's quest toward silence the spiritual-sounding name she once gave it, "the White Exploit" (922).

Dickinson's Gothic Poems Challenge Social Order

Joan Kirby

Joan Kirby, the senior research fellow in Interdisciplinary Women's Studies, Gender, and Sexuality at Macquarie University in Sydney, Australia, is author of The American Model *as well as journal articles on Emily Dickinson.*

Death is a prominent part of the nineteenth-century gothic mode, including madness, ghosts, monsters, prisons, zombies, and taboos. In this excerpt Kirby asserts that, in many of her death poems, Dickinson reveals her gothicism in her macabre preoccupation with corpses. Kirby explores the issue of the walking dead and death as a welcomed liberation. In the poem "I am alive—I guess," the speaker gives the impression that she will only have her own identity in death. In "Because I could not stop for Death," the speaker is driven by her suitor to marriage, a state of life-in-death. In some death poems, death, as the great leveler, brings with it freedom from oppressive order, rank, and gender roles.

Emily Dickinson's gothic poems are perhaps her most startling challenge to the symbolic order. They are transgressive poems of great energy which explore taboo states usually excluded from consideration. In these poems the speakers spare the reader no excess in their relish of the macabre, as a selection of first lines suggests: 'As by the dead we love to sit' (88); 'Do People moulder equally,/ They bury, in the Grave?'

(432) or 'If I may have it, when it's dead.' (577) In many poems, the dead simply refuse to lie down; witty, garrulous corpses relentlessly address the reader from deathbed or grave: "Twas just this time, last year, I died' (445); 'I heard a Fly buzz—when I died—' (465); 'I died for Beauty—' (449). . . .

Death Poems Challenge the Social Order

The Gothic poems fall into three main categories: those in which the speaker encounters unknown forces within the self; those in which the walking dead are women and continue Dickinson's explorations of gender; and those in which death is welcomed as a liberation from the confinements of the symbolic order. These poems challenge the ideals and propriety of the social order; they are disturbing because they question the certainty and rightness of its interpretations of the world. Madness suggests that there are forces within that are beyond its jurisdiction; human identity is not ultimately fixed, coherent, controlled, knowable. The dissolution of death is a permanent reminder of the fragility and artificiality of the social order and its rigid conventions.

Dickinson and Gothic Womanhood

In Dickinson's poetry, there is often a fine borderline between gothic poems and poems of gender in which powerless female speakers are menaced by the constant risk of violation and imminent death. The gothic has always been a genre associated with women writers. . . . Poem 470 'I am alive—I guess—'; Poem 512 'The Soul has Bandaged moments' and Poem 712 'Because I could not stop for Death—' suggest that the various stages of womanhood in the symbolic order are deathly.

In Poem, 470 the speaker is one of the living dead, unable to determine whether she is alive or dead. Only the ability to imagine herself lying in a coffin in the 'parlor' convinces her that she must be alive, but it is a curiously cheerless recognition. . . .

I am alive—I guess—

The Branches on my Hand

Are full of Morning Glory—

And at my finger's end—

The Carmine—tingles warm—

And if I hold a Glass

Across my Mouth—it blurs it—

Physician's—proof of Breath—

I am alive—because

I am not in a Room—

The Parlor—Commonly—it is—

So Visitors may come—

And lean—and view it sidewise—

And add "How cold—it grew"—

And "Was it conscious—when it stepped

In Immortality?"

I am alive—because—

I do not own a House—

Entitled to myself—precise—

And fitting no one else—

And marked my Girlhood's name—

So Visitors may know

Which Door is mine—and not mistake—

And try another Key—

How good—to be alive!

How infinite—to be

Alive—two-fold—The Birth I had—

And this—besides, in—Thee!

The speaker is disassociated from her body and before her eyes it seems to be turning into other forms of matter; the 'Branches' on her hand are 'full of Morning Glory' and the fingers tipped with 'Carmine' suggest a further metamorphosis; carmine is a crimson colour made from the body of insects (cochineal). There is a blurring of animal, vegetable, insect. She hypothesises that she is alive because she is not laid out in the 'parlor' so visitors, may view her body. However, the undifferentiation of death is hers in life; she does not 'own a House—/ Entitled to myself' and marked with her 'Girlhood's name'. In life she is curiously unhoused and not at home. Indeed in death it seems she would have more identity than in life; she would have a space of her own and it would bear her own name.

After the listless, sombre tone of the first six stanzas the forced cheer of the last stanza rings unconvincing: 'How good—to be alive!/ How infinite—to be/ Alive—two-fold— The Birth I had—/And this—besides, in—Thee!' The last stanza suggests that the speaker is a girl betrothed, one about to be 'Born—Bridalled—Shrouded—/ In a Day—' (1072). The betrothal has brought her a sense of life that, as in Poem 646 'I think to Live—may be a Bliss', is a cancellation of the person she was before. This new life, being born in another, is not life either: both girl and wife lack autonomy. . . .

Courtship and Marriage Are Death for a Woman

Dickinson's most famous Poem 712 'Because I could not stop for Death—' deals with a similar moment in which a woman is severed from her chosen tasks and carried off by an anonymous gentleman called 'Death'. Once again the fair theme of love is associated with 'a thought so mean'. However, this

Illustration of a bride, 1815. Joan Kirby argues that Emily Dickinson saw marriage as a type of death, and actual death as liberation from oppressive gender roles. © Historical Picture Archive/Corbis.

poem makes explicit the fact that the advent of the gentleman caller is nothing short of death for the woman. While this poem is usually read as a poem about death, revealing

Dickinson's playfully macabre vision of death as a gentleman caller, it is a poem that identifies the gentleman caller as death; for him woman is expected to put away both her labour and her leisure. Like the woman in Poem 732 she is expected to rise 'to His Requirement' and drop 'The Playthings of Her Life/ To take the honorable Work/ Of Woman, and of Wife—'.

Because I could not stop for Death—

He kindly stopped for me—

The Carriage held but just Ourselves—

And Immortality.

We slowly drove—He knew no haste

And I had put away

My labor and my leisure too,

For His Civility—

We passed the School, where Children strove

At Recess—in the Ring—

We passed the Fields of Gazing Grain—

We passed the Setting Sun—

Or rather—He passed Us—

The Dews drew quivering and chill—

For only Gossamer, my Gown—

My Tippet—only Tulle—

We paused before a House that seemed

A Swelling of the Ground—

The Roof was scarcely visible—

The Cornice—in the Ground—

Since then—'tis Centuries—and yet

Feels shorter than the Day

I first surmised the Horses' Heads

Were toward Eternity—

The first stanza suggests that the female speaker is so deeply engaged in her own life that she does not wish to stop, but it also suggests the passivity of female desire. Courting is a male prerogative; she must wait to be called upon, but once chosen a surrender that is both quick and total is expected. She must give up her work and her leisure 'For His Civility'. He has all the privileges of authority; he nominates the time of execution but is regarded as 'kindly' and civil. That the death coach contains the new couple—'And Immortality'—suggests something of the enormous duration of the marriage journey. However, it also suggests that male authority extends into eternity; both earthly life and after life are in his hands; indeed that hypothesis underpins his authority here.

The second stanza highlights the slowness and solemnity of this journey to a bridal house that strongly resembles a grave. Like the anonymous 'He' in Poem 315 'He fumbles at your Soul', 'He knew no haste'. She is assumed to have no interest or activity separate from his. Rather like the woman in Poem 273 'He put the Belt around my life—', she begins to sense her 'Lifetime folding up—'. As the journey progresses the speaker becomes increasingly aware that she has lost all agency and volition. Like the woman in Poem 443 her 'ticking' has stopped. The fields of grain are 'gazing' at her; the setting sun 'passed Us'. In her bridal finery she experiences a mortal chill: 'For only Gossamer, my Gown—/ My Tippet—only Tulle—'. Indeed the fine silk veil around her neck is a kind of noose; like the bride in Poem 1072 she is 'Born—Bridalled— Shrouded—/ In a day—'. The wedding house turns out to be her grave; it is lowly and scarcely undifferentiated from the ground. Since this deathly bridal day, it seems like 'Centuries' and 'Eternity'. Dickinson's poem suggests the eternity of death-in-life endured after marriage. . . .

Death as Woman's Insurrection— Not Ressurrection

Dickinson's most striking gothic poems are those in which the dead address the speaker from deathbed or grave. These poems bear out Gillian Beer's view that 'Ghost stories are to do with the insurrection, not the resurrection of the dead.' . . . It goes without saying that these poems are disconcerting. Death is the ultimate taboo and the corpse 'the ultimate impurity', 'the most sickening waste'. Yet Dickinson's speakers provocatively play on graves, sit by the dead, wonder if corpses moulder equally. In drawing near the corpse, the object that marks the limit between life and death, Dickinson invokes a place that is outside the rule of the symbolic order. In these poems, death marks the dissolution of the social order and becomes an emblem of liberation from its oppressive and artificial conventions. The corpse highlights the frailty of the symbolic order. As Julia Kristeva writes, a 'decaying body, lifeless, completely turned into dejection, blurred between the inanimate and the inorganic . . . the corpse represents fundamental pollution.' It is 'above all the opposite of the spiritual, of the symbolic, and of divine law.'

In Poem 465 Dickinson presents a speaker beyond the limit of the symbolic order; she has 'Signed away/What portion of me be/ Assignable—' and is henceforth to nature, a decomposing body subject only to the fly. The poem highlights the radical distance between the dying, who awaits the dissolution of the human into the undifferentiated matter of the corpse, and the living, who remain entirely bound up in the trappings of the social order, property, keepsakes, and the law of the father—'the King' who is to be 'witnessed—in the Room—' . . . .

At the moment of death, the speaker's attention is deflected by the buzz of a fly, lowly earthly representative of physical decay. For the dying person that simple presence erases all other concerns, social and religious alike. However, the living reaffirm their allegiance to the symbolic order. They turn their attention away from the dying person and what is represented by death to an affirmation of their faith; they prepare themselves to witness God's presence in the room, his taking of the dying person.

While the living await the 'King' and the re-inscription of the social order, the dying person awaits the fly and a decomposition of the self into corporeal waste. . . .

Death Obliterates Social Order

The buzzing fly blocks out the light of distinction and differentiation. The buzz of the fly is the antithesis of human language with its discrete units of modulated sounds. That the blue of the sky is transposed to the buzz of the fly suggests a further scrambling of the senses. Indeed the windows fail, which suggests a total breakdown of the social framing of experience. Windows are artificial barriers between inside and outside, nature and culture; windows frame and limit vision. However, in death the social framing of experience ends. There is darkness and a dissolution of all the restricting categories and hierarchies on which the social order is based. . . .

In many poems the speakers see death as liberation from the repressive confines of the symbolic order. As the speaker in Poem 1323 says, 'I never hear that one is dead/Without the chance of Life/ Afresh annihilating me'. Death is a leveller; in death there is no hierarchy, no distinction. . . .

The pull toward death is like a satyr's invitation to misrule and carnival, to the dissolution of fixed identity, and to some new and daring birth. . . .

Dickinson's gothic poems evoke a carnivalesque world of misrule where all is topsy turvy. There is an exploration of the forbidden and a delight in excess.

Dickinson's Depiction of the Bereaved Is Varied

Paul Ferlazzo

Paul Ferlazzo is a professor at Michigan State University. He has published on Walt Whitman, Henry Thoreau, and Carl Sandburg.

Ferlazzo maintains Emily Dickinson's view of death as seen in her poetry is ambiguous in her more than six hundred poems on death. Is death a relief from life's pain? Or a trick played on humankind? One group of these poems is on the process of observing the dead. Sometimes the viewer feels honored and obligated to be a witness. In other cases witnessing death is shown to give one the courage to prepare for one's own death. Dickinson's concern in these poems is for the bereaved and how they can cope with the death of loved ones by becoming overwhelmed with death rituals, such as funerals. They are also in shock, in "benumbed coolness," and they become mechanical. Moreover, the death of a loved one results in guilt and tests the faith of those who are left behind. Although death is sometimes linked to royalty, Dickinson sees it as the great equalizer, treating low and high ranks the same.

Closely related to Emily Dickinson's religious poetry are her poems on the subject of death. In both she seeks answers to final questions about existence, purpose, and destiny; in both she boldly pursues a sense of understanding wherever the answer may lead, sometimes at the expense of peace and consolation. She was painfully aware, too, that death is the secret gateway to the other side where once and for all her doubts about religious matters would either vanish or be confirmed. An implicit aim in much of her death poetry is to risk getting close to the secret of death in the hope that she might glimpse what lies beyond. Sometimes, however, the thought of death strikes terror so deeply into her soul that she shuns the vicious trick played on unassuming mankind by a despotic God. At certain moments, death can become for Dickinson a welcome relief from pain, thought, and instability.

In almost six hundred poems she explored the nature of death as completely as any American poet ever dared. Her poems range over the physical as well as the psychological and emotional aspects of death. She looked at death from the point of view of both the living and the dying. She went so far as to imagine her own death, the loss of her own body, and the journey of her soul to the unknown. Finally, she personified death and breathed so much complexity and power of character into him that he became one of American literature's protean figures. . . .

Seeing the Lively Past of the Dying

We begin to see Dickinson's special achievement in the poem "She lay as if at play" in which she transforms the platitudes and conventions of funeral writing into significant poetry:

> She lay as if at play
>
> Her life had leaped away—
>
> Intending to return—
>
> But not so soon—
>
> Her merry Arms, half dropt—
>
> As if for lull of sport—
>
> An instant had forgot—

The Trick to start—

Her dancing Eyes—ajar—

As if their Owner were

Still sparkling through

For fun—at you—

Her Morning at the door—

Devising, I am sure—

To force her sleep—

So light—so deep—

(P, 369; I, 294)

The death of a child is a pitiable occurrence which could easily lend itself in the hands of a lesser artist to maudlin commentaries on the idealization of innocence and youth, as well as to stock characterizations of the weeping mother or of the blackhearted villain, death. But Dickinson expertly adjusts the music and images of her poem to avoid the sentimental; and, to gain the reader's compassion, she focuses on the girl, her vitality and playfulness. . . .

In almost every line there is a word which, while it applies to the attitude of the lifeless body, also suggests the energy and activity of the girl when she was living: "play," "leaped," "merry," "sport," "instant," "trick," "start," "dancing," "sparkling," "fun," "devising," "light." The poem becomes, then, not so much a poem about death or about a dead girl as a tribute to life, to the life and personality of the young girl. Our sympathies are engaged not by playing upon our morbid curiosities but by engaging our understanding and appreciation for the beauty of this young girl when she was alive.

Emily Dickinson considered it a necessity and an honor to be present at the bedside of a loved one about to die. In "The

A 1861 funeral procession in Boston—honoring the Civil War dead of the Sixth Massachusetts Infantry Regiment—illustrates what Dickinson calls "that Dark Parade—/ Of Tassels—and of Coaches." © Corbis.

World—feels dusty/When we stop to Die," she expresses her wish to be the one chosen to bring comfort during the final moments of life: . . . .

In another poem she pleads with a loved one that she be notified of impending death:

Promise This—When You be Dying—

Some shall summon Me—

Mine belong Your latest Sighing—

Mine—to Belt Your Eye—. . . .

The Positive Value of Witnessing Death

But, in another poem, witnessing death has a value for the living that is rational and more accessible to the reader. It is a lesson in courage that frees us from the fear of death and prepares us for the moment when we ourselves shall die:

'Tis so appalling—it exhilarates—

So over Horror, it half Captivates—

The Soul stares after it, secure—

To know the worst, leaves no dread more—

To scan a Ghost, is faint—

But grappling, conquers it—

How easy, Torment, now—

Suspense kept sawing so—

Watching how a death happens removes both the suspense and the fear of it that existed in imagined versions of death. "Looking at Death, is Dying" she says later in the poem; and she suggests how, like watching a theatrical tragedy, we may be purged of our fear and set free to enjoy life:

It sets the Fright at liberty—

And Terror's free—

Gay, Ghastly, Holiday!

(P, 281; I, 200–201)

But the closing line of the poem, by juxtaposing "gay" and "ghastly," reminds us how uneasy our freedom is, since it can never completely put aside the specter of death. . . .

Focus on the Bereaved

In other poems, Dickinson shifted her attention from the dying to the living; and she focused on those left behind who had to cope with sorrow and learn to readjust their lives. In "There's been a Death, in the Opposite House" (P, 389; I, 306–7), Dickinson observes how humans try to divert their suffering and loss through ritual and ceremony. Looking from her window at the house across the road, she knows "by the numb look/Such Houses have" that someone has died. The sudden increase in activity in the house is the formal and mechanical kind that death imposes on the distressed living:

The Neighbors rustle in and out—

The Doctor—drives away—

A Window opens like a Pod—

Abrupt—mechanically—

Somebody flings a Mattress out—

The Children hurry by—

Other solemn figures arrive and behave with typically ceremonious detachment: the minister who "goes stiffly in," the milliner, and "the Man/Of the Appalling Trade." After witnessing the regularized, hushed behavior surrounding the house, the narrator observes:

There'll be that Dark Parade—

Of Tassels—and of Coaches—soon—

It's easy as a Sign—

The Intuition of the News—

In just a Country Town—

In another poem the instinctive formality of the living, when confronted with death, approaches a condition of nearly total emotional suppression. . . .

In addition, the uniformly toneless description of the entire event contributes to the strained objectivity and benumbed coolness Dickinson is striving to maintain. The poem opens by indicating how the presence of death makes the ordinary appear extraordinary; the unseen, glaring:

The last Night that She lived

It was a Common Night

Except the Dying—this to Us

Made Nature different

We noticed smallest things—

Things overlooked before

By this great light upon our Minds

Italicized—as 'twere.

The observers can do little but pass in and out of the sick room and feel "a Blame/That Others could exist/While She must finish quite." They wait in silence while she passes away, "Too jostled were Our Souls to speak." When the moment of death passes, the mourners routinely adjust the deceased and are left with an overwhelming emptiness as they try to understand the meaning of what has happened:

And We—We placed the Hair—

And drew the Head erect—

And then an awful leisure was

Belief to regulate—

Speaking of this last stanza, Brita Lindberg-Seyersted has justly observed that "The repetition of 'We' suggests the mechanical movements of the mourners and perhaps also the faltering voice of one describing the last night that the beloved woman lived." The mourners are left to face their own crisis—a crisis of faith—and to try to regulate their belief to accept the death of a dearly loved.

Death's Implications in a World Without Meaning

Wendy Martin

Professor and chair of English at Claremont Graduate School, Wendy Martin founded and edits the journal Women's Studies. *She is the author of many books, including* Emily Dickinson *and* The Cambridge Companion to Emily Dickinson.

Martin argues that Dickinson's views of death and the afterlife were shaped by her rebellion against conventional religion, including her growing doubts about the divinity of Jesus, the traditional Christian God, and the whole idea of salvation, damnation, and the afterlife. One first sees a hint of this in her resistance to a religious revival at Mount Holyoke. Her poetry shows that she held the world, nature, and life on earth to be of prime importance. Yet she was fascinated with the implications of death in what seemed a godless universe without meaning. Death brought up the puzzle of the body's relationship to the soul. She believed that the dead lived not in heaven or hell but in the memory of the living. Martin writes that ultimately Dickinson saw death as an adventure, but that she continued to celebrate earthly existence and the revelation we receive in the living moment.

As a young woman Emily Dickinson experienced a series of conflicts with powerful male figures from which she gained a sense of herself as an independent thinker and writer.

In order to achieve psychological and artistic autonomy, she had to undergo a "civil war" of the self against the very authorities—religious, familial, literary—she sometimes sought to follow.

The Battle for Self Reliance

Her first skirmish in the battle for self-reliance was with the traditional religious concept of an all-powerful God who laid claim to her soul. As an adolescent she resisted being converted during the religious revival that swept through Mount Holyoke Seminary where she was sent to school from 1847 to 1848. In her sermons the headmistress, Mary Lyons, skillfully applied the fire-and-brimstone rhetoric used a century earlier by the Puritan preacher Jonathan Edwards. Most of Dickinson's classmates responded, but Dickinson remained impenitent. For meeting after meeting, she was the only student described as having "no hope" of salvation. Even the conversions of her father and sister in the revival in Amherst in 1850 did not sway her, and she wrote to her close friend, Abiah Root, "I am standing alone in rebellion."

For Dickinson, submission to Christ as her "Master" meant relinquishing her attachment to life on earth as well as her individuality. After more than a year of spiritual turmoil, she admitted to Abiah, "I know not why, I feel that the world holds a predominant place in my affections, I do not feel I could give up all for Christ, were I called to die," But even though she resolutely resisted conversion, Dickinson felt extraordinarily guilty: "I am one of the lingering *bad* ones, and so do I slink away, and pause, and ponder, and ponder, and pause, and do work without knowing why—not surely for *this* brief world, and more sure it is not for Heaven." Alternating between self-possession and self-abnegation, Emily Dickinson ultimately embraced the risks and rewards of spiritual autonomy. "The shore is safer," she wrote to Abiah Root in December 1850, "but I love to buffet the sea."

Illustration of an 1851 revival meeting in Eastham, Massachusetts, which attracted more than five thousand attendees. Emily Dickinson resisted the revivalist movement when it swept Mount Holyoke, even after her father and sister converted in 1850. © Corbis.

Ultimately, Emily Dickinson rejected a theology based on the absolutes of salvation and damnation, vice and virtue, and instead accepted the experiential discontinuity and linguistic ambiguity that characterized her life. . . .

The Joy of Nature and the Horror of Death

She insisted on reverence for daily life: "O Matchless Earth. We underrate the chance to dwell in thee." A close family friend, Clara Newman Turner, observed that Dickinson was profoundly attuned to nature's rhythms: "Her events were the coming of the first birds;—the bursting of a young chrysalis;—the detection of the first fascinating spring fuzz of green in the air—the wonderful opening of the new world in every little flower; an unusual sunset; the autumn changes—and the inexhaustible life." Reshaping the Puritan ideal of the city on a hill into a vision in which "Nature is Heaven," she said, "I find ecstasy in living—the mere sense of living is joy enough."

Nothing was more frightening or fascinating to Emily Dickinson than death, which she referred to as the "flood subject." Throughout her life she grieved deeply for the loss of those she loved. As an adolescent, she was profoundly depressed by the deaths of her friend Sophia Holland from consumption and of Austin's friend Frazer Stearns who was killed in the Civil War. When her Aunt Lavinia died in 1860, Emily Dickinson wrote:

> Blessed Aunt Lavinia now; all the world goes out.... I sob and cry till I can hardly see my way 'round the house again; ... it is dark and strange to think of summer afterward: how she loved the summer; the birds keep singing just the same. Oh! the thoughtless birds.

Her father's death fifteen years later rekindled deep anxieties about the fate of the soul:

> I dream about father every night, always a different dream, and forget what I am doing daytimes, wondering where he is. Without any body, I keep thinking, what kind can that be?

This emotional crisis had important metaphysical implications—in a universe without God, what principles gave meaning to life and death? The epistemological and theological complexities in the questions of the existence of an all-powerful god and the relationship of the spirit to the flesh, or the mind/body problem, repeatedly surface in Dickinson's work, and her best poetry expresses the intense anxiety she experienced in her effort to resolve these issues. Ultimately, Emily Dickinson realized that life after death consists of the memories of the deceased cherished by their loved ones: "Show me eternity, and I'll show you memory," she declared.

During her mother's invalidism, Dickinson learned lessons daily about physical frailty and the process of dying. In the final phases of her mother's illness, Dickinson seems to have accepted death as an inevitable conclusion of life:

> Brave Vinnie is well—Mother does not yet stand alone and
> fears she never shall walk, but I tell her we all shall fly so
> soon, not to let it grieve her, and what indeed is Earth but a
> Nest, from whose rim we are all falling?

When Emily Norcross Dickinson died, her daughter wrote, "She slipped from our fingers like a flake gathered by the wind, and now part of the drift called 'the infinite.'" When her much-loved eight-year-old nephew Gilbert died in 1883, Dickinson succumbed to "nervous prostration" and experienced a "revenge of the nerves." Upon the death of Otis Lord, a family friend with whom Emily Dickinson had a long-distance courtship from 1881 until 1884, her profound sorrow deepened her understanding of her own mortality.

Some of Dickinson's most powerful poems express her firmly held conviction that life cannot be fully comprehended without an understanding of death:

> The Zeroes—taught us—Phosphorus—
>
> We learned to like the Fire
>
> By playing Glaciers—when a Boy—
>
> And Tinder—guessed—by power
>
> Of Opposite—to balance Odd—
>
> If White—a Red—must be!
>
> Paralysis—our Primer—dumb—
>
> Unto Vitality!
>
> (#689)

Paralleling Opposite; Death as Adventure

Paralleling life and death, these opposites—heat and cold, light and dark, health and sickness—exist in a reciprocal relationship creating meaning for each other. For Dickinson, this "Compound Vision," "the Finite—furnished/ With the Infinite," lends depth and meaning to the present moment. Eternity is not a specific destination but the enfolding present, or, as she observed, "Forever—is composed of Nows—"

Repeatedly, Dickinson insists that it is a mistake to represent the concept of eternity as a place: "The Blunder is in estimate./ Eternity is there/ We say, as of a Station" (#1684). Dickinson often uses the word "estimate" to underscore the misguided efforts to measure and delimit existence: "I fear we think too lightly of the gift of mortality, which, too gigantic to comprehend, certainly cannot be estimated," she wrote when Samuel Bowles was dying.

Ultimately, Emily Dickinson learned to see death as an "Adventure," concluding that "Dying is a wild Night and a new Road." With her acceptance of the inevitability of death came a deepened reverence for life:

Did life's penurious length

Italicize its sweetness,

The men that daily live

Would stand so deep in joy

That it would clog the cogs

Of that revolving reason

Whose esoteric belt

Protects our sanity.

(#1717)

Anticipating modernists [poets] like Marianne Moore, Theodore Roethke, Wallace Stevens, and William Carlos Williams, Dickinson believed that death intensifies life: "Uncertain lease—develops lustre/ On Time," or as she observed in another poem, "That it will never come again/ Is what makes life so sweet."

A Rejection of Salvation

Instead of relying on the comforts of the conventional religious doctrine, Emily Dickinson responded to mortality by creating a cosmology that was centered on nurturance and generativity. Her playful working of the Trinity expresses her priorities: "In the name of the Bee—/ And of the Butterfly—/ And of the Breeze—Amen!" Sardonically remarking that she "wished the faith of the Fathers didn't wear blue Brogans and carry Umbrellas," Dickinson often parodied religious pieties and took an ironic view of orthodox beliefs: "The Bible is an antique Volume—/ Written by faded Men." With no theological certainty to comfort her, Dickinson was sustained by her love of family, friends, and nature. Love, not power, was at the core of Dickinson's cosmology: "Pardon my sanity in a world *in*sane, and love me if you will, for I had rather *be* loved than to be called a King in earth, or a lord in Heaven," she wrote to Elizabeth Holland in 1856. For her, the tenderness embedded in the female tradition was superior to the control and power traditionally prized by men.

Describing herself as being on "an errand from the heart," Dickinson demonstrated extraordinary courage in her rejection of the promise of salvation and the threat of damnation and in her celebration of earthly existence. Describing her life, Emily Dickinson wrote her own epitaph:

But awed beyond my errand—

I worshipped—did not "pray"

The rebellious girl who dared to pick "Satan's flowers" became a major poet who was rewarded with the revelation of the moment.

Frost as Death in Dickinson's Poems

Patrick J. Keane

Patrick J. Keane, Professor Emeritus at Le Moyne College, is a prolific author of literary studies, including books on Ralph Waldo Emerson, William Butler Yeats, Robert Graves, and Samuel Taylor Coleridge.

In the following viewpoint Keane speculates on Emily Dickinson's image of death as it is linked to frost in many poems. In poem 1624, however, death is associated with both frost and sun. Both are assassins whose destructive actions are approved by God. The question the presence of the sun raises is whether frost or death is part of nature's cycle of dying and rebirth or whether frost is a death-bringer with only negative connotations. It appears to be identified, not with faith and resurrection, but with terror, utter ruin, and Satan. Some critics argue that frost and God (the onlooker) are just the spiritual and psychological agents that must appear before renewal can take place. But Keane argues that death and God bring on a finality that makes one's "blood run cold."

That destruction by Nature is accomplished in the first quatrain of "Apparently with no surprise." In the second, we encounter all three of the poem's dramatically described agents: "the blonde Assassin," that "Approving God," and the Sun that "proceeds unmoved." . . .

Patrick J. Keane, *Divine Design and the Problem with Suffering*. Columbia: University of Missouri Press, 2008. Copyright © 2008 by The Curators of the University of Missouri. All rights reserved. Reproduced by permission. Incorporated Emily Dickinson poems from *The Poems of Emily Dickinson*, The Belknap Press of Harvard University Press. Copyright © 1951, 1955, 1979, 1983 by the President and Fellows of Harvard College. Reprinted by permission of the Trustees of Amherst College.

Frost as Death

Frost, though a cold killer, is *not* a "dark" destroyer. Instead, this "blonde Assassin" is a pale rider, an agent of the destruction of beauty that is itself luminously beautiful—pure, prismatic, pristine, glistening.

It is the fusion of beauty with lethality that is most stressed in Dickinson's poems about frost, poems that typically associate frost with death, natural and human. In one poem, in which living beauty becomes petrified, the speaker knows a place

> where Summer strives
>
> With such a practiced Frosty—
>
> She—each year—leads her Daisies back—
>
> Recording—briefly—"Lost"—

But the promise of vernal rebirth implicit in the hopeful adverb *briefly* is not always fulfilled, as suggested by the opening line's strenuous and perhaps impotent *striving*. When spring's South wind is more turbulent than usual (echoing "strives," it "stirs" the ponds and "struggles" in the lanes), Summer's "Heart misgives her for her Vow," and she "pours" soft elegiac "Refrains"

> Into the lap of Adamant—
>
> And spices—and the Dew—
>
> That stiffens quietly to Quartz
>
> Upon her Amber Shoe—(337)

In another poem, Frost's caress is intimate yet fatal. This "Visitor in Marl" (normally, fertilizing loam, but here, as Judith Farr has suggested, a possible play on the contraction for "marble," or gravestone) "influences Flowers—/ Till they are orderly as Busts—/ And elegant—as Glass—." But the price of this crystallization of flowers into aesthetic artifacts goes beyond abandonment by a bold but transient lover. In this garden version of an *aubade*, the male Frost

> visits in the Night—
>
> And just before the Sun—
>
> Concludes his glistening interview—
>
> Caresses—and is gone—
>
> But whom his fingers touched—
>
> And where his feet have run
>
> And whatsoever Mouth he kissed—
>
> Is as it had not been. (391)

The "sexual dimension" . . . detected in "Apparently with no surprise" is here overt. In both poems, the Frost's "influence," before his "glistening interview" is concluded by the melting rays of the sun, is death, indeed nullification. Any flower caressed and sensuously kissed by this *homme fatale* is "*as if it had not been*": a finality paralleling the more brutal eradication by the beheading Assassin. Natural mutability, the destruction of beauty in nature, is always a human theme as well, repeatedly expressed by Dickinson in terms of frost's assault on flowers. Poems such as "A Visitor in Marl" and "Apparently with no surprise" describe, as Judith Farr says, "the killing of her flowers, an event that always seemed to her like murder." . . . In Dickinson's poem, "The Frost was never seen—/ If met, too rapid past"; still, the "Flowers" are the first to notice a "Stranger hovering round,"

> A Symptom of alarm
>
> In Villages remotely set
>
> But search effaces him
>
> Till some retrieveless Night

Our Vigilance at ease

The Garden gets the only shot

That never could be traced.

This alien Frost, a kind of sniper haunting the outskirts armed with lethal force, is "never seen" until it is too late, and then becomes emblematic of all the mysterious forces of earth and air:

Unproved is much we know—

Unknown the worst we fear—

Of Strangers is the Earth the Inn

Of Secrets is the Air—

To analyze perhaps

A Philip would prefer

But Labor vaster than myself

I find it to infer. (1202)

Death as an Insoluble Mystery

The apostle Philip might seek demonstrable evidence of the invisible God ("Lord, show us the Father"), even though Jesus had just said, "If ye had known me, ye should have known my Father also" (John 14:7–9). But Emily Dickinson knows that ultimate mysteries are insoluble. God working through frost in the garden induces not faith but fear, and terrifying inferences of inscrutable, destructive power rather than comforting religious revelation.

In "The Frost of Death was on the Pane," our efforts to fight "Mortality" are futile, defeated by a frigid force at once lethal, serpentine, and satanic. Despite our struggle to protect the feminine "passive Flower," the aggressive Frost, an insidious intruder, began "to crawl":

We pried him back

Ourselves we wedged

Himself and her between,

Yet easy as the narrow Snake

He forked his way along.

Till all her helpless beauty bent

And then our wrath begun—

We hunted him to his Ravine

We chased him to his Den—

We hated Death and hated Life

And nowhere was to go—

Than Sea and continent there is

A larger—it is Woe. (1136)

The passionate intensity of the poem, which Alfred Habegger considers Dickinson's "most wrathful lyric," may in part be attributable to her reaction to the serious illness and death at this time (1866) of a young woman friend. The inexorable frost that "bends" and destroys "helpless beauty" in the form of a flower evokes a tragic version of the romance motif. To that motif, in which a "helpless" maiden cannot be saved, the final stanza, stressing "Woe" (a *human sorrow* more immense than "Sea and continent"), adds a vision from Revelation: "Woe to the inhabiters of the earth and of the sea! For the devil has come down to you in great wrath" (Rev. 12:12). Though she does not cite this biblical passage, Paula Bennett perceptively depicts the forces at work not only in *this* poem but, I would add, also in "Apparently with no surprise" and "Like Time's insidious wrinkle" (neither of which she discusses). "Like a Satanic trinity," she writes, the snake is death, frost, and (presumably) the devil in one. As such, it epitomizes the destructive potential which Dickinson seems to have believed was latent in all forms of masculine power, including God's. It is God, after all, who ordains frost, death, and snake. They are the instruments of His will, the means through which His ordination comes to pass.

The Male Frost "Dishevels" Beauty

The other poem . . . , though "Shakespearean" in motif, may also be covertly Miltonic. Here Frost "dishevels" rather than "beheads," though mutability merges with mortality:

Like Time's insidious wrinkle

On a beloved's Face

We clutch the Grace the tighter

Though we resent the crease.

The *Frost himself so comely*

Dishevels every prime

Asserting from his Prism

That none can punish him. (1236; italics added). . .

In Dickinson's poem, the male force, the Frost, "dishevels" beauty, beauty which—whatever its human implications—is in the first place a *flower*. . . .

To refocus . . . questions in terms of the Frost's beheading of the Flower in "Apparently with no surprise": is it emblematic of a pattern essentially tragic or providential, an illustration of meaningless destruction or of purposive "Design"? And if it *is* "designed," what does that tell us about the Designer? The killing Frost, the lethal headsman in this memorable scene, exemplifies what Yeats called (in "A Prayer for My Daughter") "the murderous innocence" of nature. It destroys in "accidental power," but it is acting, presumably, as the agent of the *Supreme* Power, by whose divine "breath," according to Job 37:10, "frost is given." But if frost is ambiguous in Job and one of the glories of a providential God in Psalms (147:16), it seems a sign of his ruthlessness in "Apparently with no surprise." As an ambassador of death, Frost is an assassin sent forth at the behest, or with the acquiescence, of God, who is himself described as an "Assassin" in poem 1102. The unmoved Sun also performs its measurement "for" this "*Approving* God." Echoing the initial "*Apparently*," this "*Approving*" Deity ("apparently") sanctions the whole of the drama we have just witnessed—a garden scene that at first seems . . . limited . . . but which . . . confronts us with the human and even cosmic mysteries presented earlier.

All the players in Dickinson's drama—ascending hierarchically from unsurprised Flower to powerful Frost to measuring Sun to approving God—take the beheading casually and in stride. Some readers do as well. Others find the poem disturbing, even shocking. Some may detect in the poem's measured tone and metrical regularity support for an argument that Dickinson herself observes the process she describes with the same equanimity exhibited, in their different ways, by Flower, Frost, Sun, and God. For such readers, the poem conveys an archetypal sense, ranging from the botanical through the psychological to the spiritual, that destruction necessarily precedes new creation; that out of death comes life, out of evil, good. For other readers, myself included, there is the unmistakable sense that—beneath its calm, "detached" surface—the poem's tone and central act reveal Dickinson (or the poem's dramatic speaker) to be *disturbed* by what is described, and that she chooses her subject, language, and dramatic treatment with the deliberate intention of disturbing *us*.

Whichever way readers lean, the central question raised by "Apparently with no surprise" is whether the accidental beheading in the poem is a *merely* destructive act or part of a more inclusive plan, vegetative and theistic. In the world of natural process, frost is not necessarily divorced from rebirth; it can be either lethal, as it certainly seems to be in the case of a beheading Assassin, or a damaging visitation from which renewed life springs—a precursor of cyclical revival. . . .

Frost as a Negative Force

On both the natural and the human level, frost was for Dickinson a predominantly negative, deadly force—unsurprisingly for a New England gardener used to weather changeable and often cold, one also deeply affected by the many deaths she saw all around her. In the famous "After great pain, a formal feeling comes," the "Hour of Lead" is remembered, if "outlived," as a form of death: "As Freezing persons recollect the Snow—/ First—Chill—then Stupor—then the letting go—" (341). But in her poems and letters, it is not snow but, specifically, *frost* that is obsessively equated with death—often as graphically if seldom as dramatically as in the decapitation by the blonde Assassin.

In "I cannot live with you" (640), Dickinson asks how she could stand by and watch her beloved "freeze" without her own "Right of Frost—/ Death's privilege." In an earlier poem, she refers to those long dead as "The bosoms where the frost has lain / Ages beneath the mould—" (132). In an 1865 letter, she describes the grave in which Susan's sister had just buried her second child as an "ice nest" (*L* 444). In an attempt to recollect the dead, she tries to recall recently deceased friends once pleased by something one said: "You try to touch the smile, / And dip your fingers in the frost—" (509). A poem responding to the death of a fallen soldier begins: "Victory comes late—/ And is held low to freezing lips—/ Too rapt with frost / To take it—" (690). Searching for metaphors to express "Despair," she initially remarks, "It was not Frost," only to concede that, while it is "most, like Chaos," despair also resembles "Grisly frosts" that on autumn mornings "Repeal the

Beating Ground" (510). This repeal of the pulsating life of summer allies human death and despair with floral death-by-frost. . . .

"There is a flower that Bees prefer" (380) praises the purple clover, a flower both early blooming ("She doth not wait for June") and heroically "sturdy," yet doomed:

The Bravest—of the Host—

Surrendering—the Last—

Not even of Defeat—aware—

When cancelled by the Frost—

Here, as in our main poem, where a happy Flower is beheaded by a canceling Frost, it is, by clear implication, *we* who are "aware" of this sure obliteration. In both cases, especially in "Apparently with no surprise," the inexorable yet sudden, dramatic death by frost with divine approval seems, especially if "design govern in a thing so small," calculated to make our own blood run cold.

Dickinson Explored Death Unflinchingly

Bettina L. Knapp

Bettina L. Knapp taught at Hunter College. She was a widely published psychological literary critic. Her specialties included the theater, women writers, Jewish culture, multicultural studies, and myth.

Knapp says that Emily Dickinson had two conflicting selves: the daughter with a lowly place in her family and community and the young woman with an independence of mind regarding religion. This independence led her to a radical view of death as the final bringer of loss and separation from which one cannot be resurrected. Being able to sustain the conventional view of God as benevolent would have made facing death tolerable, but, for Dickinson, it would also have been a delusion. Instead she believes that death is God's joke that has gone "too far." In one poem death is the falling into nothingness. In another it obliterates time, change, and awareness. In such a state of "petrifaction," resurrection is hardly an option. The American Civil War reinforced her vision of death as evil. Her questioning of death was part of her determination to explore the unknown but with her eyes wide open.

To build a world of one's own rather than live in a state of beatitude or primary identification within the family was particularly arduous for Dickinson, considering the times in which she lived and the closeness of her family ties. Other perils were also in the offing. To step away from the known into the unknown, to reject the palliatives offered to her by organized religion, aroused in her feelings of deprivation and forfeiture, resulting in an obsessive preoccupation with death.

Loss of Faith and Anxiety over Death

The anxieties revolving around her fears of loss and separation, which death implies, may be viewed as a projection onto the outer world of an acute inner sense of hurt and disablement. Was it really her friends and relatives that she was mourning when they passed into death or moved away to other areas? Was it really their company that had been *lost* to her now that they had dropped away? Yes, to be sure. But only on a conscious level. Unconsciously, what she really dreaded was the "fall" of her own life. The panic overwhelming her was triggered by feelings of a possible dissolution of her ego, the possible stunting of her personality and an inability to develop her potential for creativity—the making a name for herself. Her repeated use in her poetry of such words as *loss, drop, fall* mirrors the terror she experienced at the thought of confronting the hurdles that would prevent her from fulfilling her life's mission. The impasses she envisaged were formidable, indeed, because her struggle was not merely to take place on an everyday level, but on a vaster scaled—like that of Job, in a metaphysical dimension.

Because she rejected the traditional beliefs and values instilled in her by her family and community, Dickinson felt empty inside, as though she were living on the edge of a precipice, on the verge of falling, dropping into, and losing herself in the fathomless and monstrous depths of an abyss. . . .

Puzzle About the Nature of God

The question of death, uppermost in her mind, would have to be probed if Dickinson were to make headway in her development as woman and poet.

I know that He exists.

Somewhere—in Silence—

He has hid his rare life

From our gross eyes.

'Tis an instant's play.

'Tis a fond Ambush—

Just to make Bliss

Earn her own surprise!

But—should the play

Prove piercing earnest—

Should the glee—glaze—

In Death's—stiff—stare—

Would not the fun

Look too expensive!

Would not the jest—

Have crawled too far! (#338) (1862)

The affirmation, in the above poem, that "He" (God) exists, is not only comforting to the narrator, but was a constant throughout Dickinson's life. What is less certain, however, is the nature of deity. If God "exists" as a transcendental, impersonal, silent, undefined power, He does not mitigate the narrator's fears. . . . He is shrouded in disguises, manifests Himself in mysterious ways, and remains hidden from the "gross eyes" and limited understanding of humankind. To endow God with qualities of benevolence is to foster illusion, the way children at play erect an "Ambush—/ Just to make Bliss" or earn "surprise." To believe in such a divinity is to give credence to a lure, a decoy, a palliative, as do the Scriptures. . . .

What of Death? she ironizes. According to the Scriptures, the passing from life to death is a wonderful experience in that it reintegrates what has once been united: mortals with their Creator. The narrator, however, no longer the naive believer she has been once, cannot accept such a blissful assumption. The pronouncement of God's existence and the metaphor of humanity's merry fantasies associated with His benevolence and compassion, are like so many childhood games or deceits. . . .

The shedding of the palliative belief in the existence of a compassionate and All-Good God who works to better humankind's earthly lot awakens the narrator to a dual and antagonistic world, with destruction and pain rampant, like so many nails stabbing her flesh. The "piercing" image also evokes her need to pierce through those barriers erected in the Scriptures, thereby increasing her perception so as better to bypass the emotional and intellectual obstacles on her path. No longer can she close her eyes and hide behind mechanisms serving only to blur her vision; she now looks at death in "earnest." Staring back with eyes wide open, the narrator observes its "glee—glaze" and "stiff—stare" and its "piercing" gaze.

Life, once a game to be played, has now been transformed: *glee* has become *glaze*. Mirth, exultant high-spirited joy, and song of children at play, are replaced by the rigid, grim, icy, unassailable stare of the perceptive individual. Disquieting though it may be, her course . . . would require a quest, a puncturing, a perforation, a transpiercing of the disguises and traps set in her path since childhood, blinding her to the reality of Death's substantiality: his "stiff—stare" and blank gaze.

Her view of death, then, is in contradiction to the scriptural: not a lover welcoming his beloved (human) back into His being, into His New Jerusalem, but destructive, macabre, duplicitous, seeking to prolong the children's spirit of "fun" and indulge them in their fantasy of eternal life. But the "jest," implying deed, wager, prank, and mockery, also smacks of sadism and, therefore, has "crawled" too far. . . .

The word *crawled* implies snake imagery—a perversion in one sense of that terrifying Satanic or Luciferian factor instrumental in awakening the curiosity of Adam and Eve, thus bringing about their Fall but also their *awakening* into life. No longer would Adam and Eve—and the narrator by implication—remain keepers of the "garden," that is, lethargic followers. . . .

The Influence of the Gothic Novel

That Dickinson should have had recourse to the macabre—stiff, stare, and the entire skeletal effect as a metaphor for death—is not surprising. The Gothic novels of Horace Walpole, Mrs. Ann Radcliffe, Jane Austen, Matthew "Monk" Lewis, and Charles Robert Maturin, popular in Europe, had their American counterparts in the works of Charles Brockden Brown, Nathaniel Hawthorne, and Edgar Allan Poe. The aforementioned novels and tales, with which Dickinson was familiar, usually took place in medieval times and in haunted castles inhabited by skeletons and other gruesome creatures intended to shock and terrorize the reader.

Nor was death in medieval times viewed as a beatific state bringing serenity and harmony to the individual, lending dignity or release from life's difficulties. Viewed by the medieval mind, and Dickinson's as well, as we shall see, death and putrescence were one and the same. Identified more and more with graveyards, ghouls, phantoms, and an angry God . . . death was a dread-arousing force.

Death Ritual as the Only Certainty

The image of the graveyard and the funeral cortege with all of the medieval allegorical ramifications is depicted in Dickinson's . . . poem:

I felt a Funeral, in my Brain,

And Mourners to and fro

Kept treading—treading—till it seemed

That Sense was breaking through—

And when they all were seated,

A Service, like a Drum—

Kept beating—beating—till I thought

My Mind was going numb—

And then I heard them lift a Box

And creak across my Soul

With those same Boots of Lead, again,

Then Space—began to toll,

As all the Heavens were a Bell,

And Being, but an Ear,

And I, and Silence, some strange Race

Wrecked, solitary, here—

And then a Plank in Reason, broke,

And I dropped down, and down—

And hit a World, at every plunge,

And Finished knowing—then. (#280)
(1861)

Funerals, the ritual commemorating the rite of passage from life to death, although a habitual sight for Dickinson, were life's only certainty. No longer viewed by the narrator as a game of hide and seek, as at the outset of the previous poem, "I felt a Funeral, in my Brain"—here is an act perpetrated by an indifferent and invisible Deity who relentlessly sees to humanity's extinction in a tragic and unequal struggle. Dickinson had been taught that God is responsible for the harmony of His Creation and that He punished humanity for having destroyed it (alluding to the notion of the original sin) by introducing death and pain into life. She also had been taught that humanity may be restored to God through Christ's grace if his Commandments, as presented in the Scriptures, are enforced, each individual committing himself to life as well as to death, working with it and toward it in joy. In the words of Jonathan Edwards: "To live with all my might, while I do live," is to maintain the precarious balance between life and death; at which Dickinson jeered with: "I felt a Funeral, in my Brain."

The Funeral cortege described in the poem is experienced objectively (in the outside world, the community participating in the ritual in good Congregationalist fashion). Because it is depicted subjectively, as narrated by the deceased, it takes on a far more harrowing note. . . .

From Death and Disorder to Poetry

Like Adam and Eve who fell into life, so the deceased, ironically, falls into death—an unending abyss, a continuous blackened pit. Alone, cut, and broken, faith no longer sustains the deceased; nor does reason, which had been substituted for it. As the product of that part of the human brain that functions in the finite world and not in the infinite sphere, it cannot cross that endless space separating earth from heaven.

Knowledge, Dickinson realizes, means, paradoxically, the acceptance of not knowing—of humility. Once the deceased (narrator) has divested herself of categories, once she has put a stop to systematizing and attempting to find coherence in life's processes—no matter the confusion or hurt that may ensue—she has stepped into a new order of her own manufacture, that of poetry. . . .

Time and time again the poet turned to the theme of death—the most fulminating of experiences for her—in order to examine its impact on her rationally, cerebrally, as well as emotionally. By exploring death as a reality, she also confronted other problems: the dichotomy existing between linear and cyclical time, mortality and immortality. . . .

In Dickinson's poem, "Safe in their Alabaster Chambers," she scornfully alters and mockingly rejects the meaning of Jesus's beatific message offering mortals eternal recompense. The statement, "Blessed are the meek: for they shall inherit the earth," is interpreted ironically by the poet: the land given to them after their demise will be sufficient for their burial (Matt. 5:5).

> Safe in their Alabaster Chambers—
>
> Untouched by Morning—
>
> And untouched by Noon—
>
> Lie the meek members of the Resurrec-
> tion—
>
> Rafter of Satin—and Roof of Stone!
>
> Grand go the Years—in the Crescent—above
> them—
>
> Worlds scoop their Arcs—
>
> And Firmaments—row—
>
> Diadems—drop—and Doges—surrender—
>
> Soundless as dots—on a Disc of Snow—
> (216) (1861)

The dead, awaiting rebirth, are "Safe" in their exquisite graves or "Alabaster Chambers." Protected from the tensions caused by doubt and indecision, they remain incarcerated in their rigid, fixed, and comfortable beliefs.

Alabaster, like stone in general, denotes unity and strength and is, therefore, not subject to biological change as are people, animals, and flowers. Symbolizing continuity and indestructible strength within nature itself, this concretion of earthly or mineral matter has its sacred side. . . .

In Dickinson's poem, however, one detects a strongly derisive note. The narrator is not dealing with ordinary stone, but with the more precious and more translucent alabaster used by the Puritan Elect who believe they are different from others and will rise again from their satin rafters (stone markers indicating the grave). That the more expensive alabaster and satin should be used by Puritans who preach virtual asceticism lends a sarcastic note to the concept. . . .

Empirical time, "Morning" and "Noon," is obliterated, the dead living in a condition of unawareness and indifference. Solipsistic beings, they exist in their narrow, unbending, closed world where change is forever shut out. . . .

The word *drop*, used by Dickinson in so many of her poems, replicates the biblical Fall both semiotically as well as phonetically; she, too, fell out of childhood and unawareness, into maturity and growing consciousness. . . .

A Sacrilegious Message

Significant as well is the vision of disintegrated bodies lying in the lugubrious Chambers. What had once been whole now exists in particles, like so many detached and disembodied silent, solitary, "dots." No longer warmed by the Sun nor by the Golden Legends that tell of patriarchal Christian compassion, the dead are ruled by the feminine Moon, an icy inanimate body viewed from within Mother Earth's sanctuary as a "Disc of Snow."

Dickinson's message is sacrilegious. It contradicts still another of Jesus's statements that seeks to instill a sense of hope in humankind: "For he must reign, till he hath put all enemies under his feet. The last enemy that shall be destroyed is death" (1 Corin. 15:26). Since everything in the new Ice Age (death) is petrification, the possibility of warmth and rebirth into life cannot occur, thus nullifying Christ's earthly mission. . . .

Unlike the faithful who believed death implicit in God's design, Dickinson rejected the thought that it was part of a divinely authorized scheme. In such poems as "It's easy to invent a Life—/God does it—every Day" (#724), Death is viewed as an Evil, a cruelty, a willful act. As for the Civil War that caused so many mortalities, it brought the very existence of organized religion into question. Though labeled a "Holy War" by Oliver Wendell Holmes, Sr., in no way did Dickinson believe there was something sacred in this conflagration.

My triumph lasted till the Drums

Had left the Dead alone

And then I dropped my Victory

And chastened stole along

To where the finished Faces

Conclusion turned on me

And then I hated Glory

And wished myself were They.

What is to be is best descried

When it has also been—

Could Prospect taste of Retrospect

The tyrannies of Men

Were Tenderer—diviner

The Transitive toward.

A Bayonet's contrition

Is nothing to the Dead. (#1227) (1872)...

Dickinson forever questioned the notion of death to the end of her days, consciously and poetically. Unshielded by buffers, refusing to veil her perceptions, she boldly explored the stages of physical decay and spiritual disorientation suffered by the departing and the departed. Like the medieval poet, François Villon, and the seventeenth-century John Donne, also obsessed with death and doubts as to salvation, Dickinson never veered from her pursuit of the unknown and the intangible.

The Freedom in Death and the Uncertainty of Immortality

Jane Donahue Eberwein

Jane Donahue Eberwein retired from Oakland University in Rochester, Michigan, where she served for many years as a distinguished professor. In addition to Emily Dickinson, she has written on Edward Taylor and other early American poets.

Eberwein writes that Dickinson considered life as occurring within a circle or globe, a "circuit world," so having a circumference. The circumference itself was death, and beyond the circumference might be freedom and immortality. Dying was the gate in the circumference that one goes through to escape the earthly confines of mortality. Death is like flying, perhaps even soaring with liberation and delight. Death could be "a wild night and a new road." But a lingering doubt remained for Dickinson that it might be nothingness rather than immortality that is in store for the dead and that consciousness ceases. Maybe the dead's only immortality resides in the memory of the living. Dickinson grieved for the "flight" of others and, at the same time, envied them their freedom. Her uncertainty is shown in thinking that a friend went to heaven but then commending him for clinging to the earth.

Given the drive of Dickinson's imagination to identify limits and explode beyond them, she could hardly have evaded death as her most constant theme. Not her "Flood subject," however; that was immortality. Reading the poems and letters on death, we must actively consider the question-

Jane Donahue Eberwein, "Dying as Drama," *Dickinson's Strategies of Limitation.* Amherst: University of Massachusetts Press, 1985. Copyright © 1985 by The University of Massachusetts Press and published by the University of Massachusetts Press.

ing about immortality that prompted her fascination. Death presented itself as a barrier, a closed door; but she insisted on trying the lock in any way she could to discover whether she could trust Christian promises of eternal and intensified life. Would the limitations that pained her in life give way to power, the gift that seemed to her to subsume the glory and dominion (L 292)? Was there a heaven to repay life's deprivations? Might human cravings for fulfillment ever be satisfied? To find out, the poet balanced herself on the perilous edge of circumference—living always in the presence of death with mind and nerves astoundingly alert.

Death as Possible Liberation

Exhilarated by the very precariousness of her perch, Dickinson responded gleefully as often as with dread. She reveled in the drama of life on the brink—particularly the brink of immortality—and she habitually represented the human condition in circumferential metaphors. When her mother, partially paralyzed by a stroke and further disabled by a broken hip, lamented the disruption of her circuit routine, the elder daughter responded in terms as characteristic as they were startling: "I tell her we all shall fly so soon, not to let it grieve her, and what indeed is Earth but a Nest, from whose rim we are all falling?" (L 619). Falling into what? Dickinson herself never felt sure, but the flight image lends hope of soaring instead—of liberation, empowerment, even of delight. . . .

Many poems and letters focus on death as the dividing line between the circuit side of existence as now experienced and the other side of mystery. In "These tested Our Horizon—" (P 886), Dickinson salutes those who probed the barrier and disappeared beyond it into "Anticipation / A Dice—a Doubt—." Only retrospect remains behind within the circuit, from within which the survivors still find the horizon a barrier to vision. As with this horizon image, Dickinson summoned other transitional metaphors . . . to represent death as circumference. She linked death explicitly with sunset in "Like her the Saints retire," (P 60), while offering a late-summer flower (the aster) and a spring bulb (the daffodil) as counter-arguments to loss. Reminded of her recent dead at the conclusion of an 1878 letter to Dr. Holland, she apologized "But I intrude on Sunset, and Father and Mr Bowles" (L 544). They had ventured into the sunset while others remained behind to watch for the sunrise, yearning for replenishment of loss and breakdown of those obstacles. . . .

It is the instinct of the circuit world to restrain wanderers and to hold them as firmly as possible within circumference. When Samuel Bowles was dying, for example, Dickinson wrote to Mrs. Holland that "Dear Mr Bowles is hesitating—God help him decide on the Mortal Side!" (L 525). But he either fell or climbed across to the other side, that of immortality or nothingness. To borrow imagery from several of her poems, he entered a door through circumference and closed it behind him. . . .

Those circumferential mental states most nearly analogous to death—despair, catatonia, madness—often aped death's physical qualities of stiffness and numbness; they created an absence within a person comparable to the distance death sets between the corpse and the circuit world. Whether they also foreshadowed mental cessation at death remained a haunting question for Emily Dickinson. What if consciousness stopped? What if awareness ceased just as the quester approached those visionary cities? The irony would be too cruel. . . .

Confined as she was within her mortal circuit though excited personally by the enticement of escape, Dickinson herself resisted the flight of others. . . .

Free of the Circuit of Life

The tension in Dickinson's own mind expresses itself in the confusion readers feel about the "Jealousy for Her" that arose

The Dickinson Homestead in Amherst, Massachusetts, where the reclusive poet lived all her life. She rarely and reluctantly ventured from it except, as Jane Donahue Eberwein writes, to escape in death. © James Marshall/Corbis.

in "The last Night that She lived" (P 1100), a particularly detailed and moving deathbed poem. Told from the perspective of one remaining in the circuit, the narrative emphasizes the impact of this woman's dying on the world she leaves behind. The "smallest things" of household routine are "Italicized" by the alertness of observation the attendants bring to her chamber. What remains after the death is sheer matter: hair to be placed neatly and the head to be positioned, but none of the consciousness that has been either transformed or obliterated. Within the circuit world of matter and time and intellectual awareness, the speaker and her fellow attendants feel a jealousy *for* the dying woman. They resent the continued existence of other people "While She must finish quite." But it seems likely that the speaker also feels a jealousy *of* the departed one. The death scene itself is revealing with the struggle for preservation all on the part of the survivors while the woman for whom they have been laboring has consented to death and allowed her life to float away upon the mystic sea.

Readiness for Death

Calvinist tradition had trained the poet to watch for signals of salvation or reprobation at the point of death, to look for evidence that Christ had come for the saint who persevered to the end. The poet's reports and questions about dying attitudes and last words, therefore, conformed to a pattern of curiosity about such things that seemed not only normal but normative to the people she knew. They shared her curiosity about each person's readiness for death. Dickinson's 1854 letter to the Reverend Edward Everett Hale, inquiring if Benjamin Newton "was willing to die, and if you think him at Home," raised predictable questions about her friend's postcircumferential status, and she need hardly have explained "I should love so much to know certainly, that he was today in Heaven" (L 153). Years later, in 1878, she reported bluntly that "Mr Bowles was not willing to die," a comment not based upon despair as to his celestial prospects but expressive of gratitude for his loyalty to the circuit world from which she so reluctantly excused him (L 553). After Bowles's death, she told Higginson that it seemed "there was no World" and no light—just "Darkness." . . .

For some people, however, flight from the circuit world seemed to offer relief, and Dickinson recognized that the dead more often tired of the living than the living of them (P 482). The persons remembered in "A poor—torn heart—a tattered heart—" (P 78) and "She bore it till the simple veins" (P 144) find dying a release as they journey beyond the sunset. And the speaker of "Where bells no more affright the morn—" (P 112) looks forward with humorous indolence to a paradise of reprieve from industriousness and its pressures. She dreams of basking forever in a heaven blessedly immune to "Father's bells" and factory whistles. Routine activity terminates with death on both sides of circumference. . . . Within the circuit, however, people have difficulty estimating "The distance that the dead have gone" (P 1742) and the impossibility of their return.

But they *have* gone, and Dickinson presents death as an adventure for the dying whether they resort to it only for purposes of escape or courageously challenge it in their quest for fulfillment. Death is her "White Exploit" (P 922) and "most profound experiment / Appointed unto Men—" (P 822). Often it seems an occasion of triumph (P 455). So ennobling is this adventure that even the circuit world accords it honor, however unwelcome its source. . . .

She regarded journeys as danger-fraught venturings into the unknown and presented every kind of travel as a prefigurement of death. . . . When her cousin, Perez Cowan, longed for death after losing his sister, Dickinson warned him that "It grieves me that you speak of Death with so much expectation. I know there is no pang like that for those we love, nor any leisure like the one they leave so closed behind them, but Dying is a wild Night and a new Road" (L 332). Fixed to the circuit world by love as well as apprehension, she admired those who undertook such journeys with a willingness to fly that surmounted their continuing affection for the world they had known. . . .

Faced with the necessity of traversing the "new Road" herself eventually, the poet often anticipated the journey and generally steeled herself for the test. She, who left her own home so rarely and reluctantly, proclaimed herself "ready to go!" if safely buckled by Christ in his carriage and escorted by him on the steep down-hill journey into the sea of mystery and beyond it (P 279). . . .

Death Offers Intensity

It was not the termination of life that excited her but the prospect of its intensification beyond circumference. The exultation she occasionally expressed at the thought of completing life's perilous journey came from anticipation of wonderful surprises beyond the limiting circuit world. . . .

Beyond death's barrier . . . lay that "great Romance" already revealed to the dead but only wonderingly intuited by the living. No wonder the poet coveted those "post mortuary gifts" and tried to glimpse the marvels promised to her but as yet foreclosed. The dead already in possession of such secrets served as lures beyond circumference, especially those departed loved ones who seemed most eager to experience the vision. Chief among these lures for Emily Dickinson was her little nephew, Gilbert, whom she visited the night of his death by typhoid fever and whose dying words lingered in her memory. "'Open the Door, open the Door, they are waiting for me,' was Gilbert's sweet command in delirium. *Who* were waiting for him, all we possess we would give to know," she told Mrs. Holland (L 873). Whatever the child meant by his imploring—whether he fantasized Christ and the angels above or only his playmates outside—he had answered the Calvinist question about his destiny in circumferential language to which his aunt was already sharply attuned. He had begged for a door to be opened, had demanded a chance for escape. . . .

The Dead Live in Memory

She told Judge Lord's executor, Benjamin Kimball, that "I once asked him what I should do for him when he was not here, referring half unconsciously to the great Expanse—In a tone italic of both Worlds 'Remember Me,' he said. I have kept his Commandment" (L 968). When Samuel Bowles died, she confided to his widow, "To remember our own Mr Bowles is all we can do" (L 532). Memory, of course, depended on the actions of the survivors; it was not controlled by the dead even when requested by them. It seemed to Emily Dickinson an almost celestial power, as she intimated in the remark that "I think Heaven will not be as good as earth, unless it bring with it that sweet power to remember, which is the Staple of

Heaven—here" (L 623) and in the exclamation to Sue, "Show me Eternity, and I will show you Memory—/ Both in one package lain / And lifted back again—" (L 912). As an almost heavenly power, remembrance seemed to her a force evading deliberate control. . . .

The lives Emily Dickinson held in contempt were those that had not been lived intensely, those that failed of growth and force. . . . The ancient person's unspent powers rebuked him. They showed him unfit to embark upon the great adventure of death. . . .

Wasted lives meant wasted dying. The poet made no attempt to follow those she scorned across circumference. But most of Dickinson's comments on the dead were charitable ones; she expressed admiration far more often than contempt. . . .

Emily Dickinson kept on speculating all her life about those possibilities "behind the Door—" (P 335) that captured her imagination. She kept inquiring about the destiny of those she loved and about her own prospects. When her mother died in November 1882, she wrote to her Norcross cousins, "We don't know where she is, though so many tell us" but went on to express a hopeful conviction: "I believe we shall in some manner be cherished by our Maker—that the One who gave us this remarkable earth has the power still farther to surprise that which He has caused. Beyond that all is silence" (L 785). "Surprise" is the key word here. We know from family reports that this woman loved surprises and secrets. When she failed to penetrate beyond circumference by her observations and role playing, she came to think of the wished-for next life as God's wonderful secret to be revealed only after death. As she told Perez Cowan in the same letter that defines death as "a wild Night and a new Road," "I suppose we are all thinking of Immortality, at times so stimulatedly that we cannot sleep. . . ."

She seems to have anticipated rather than dreaded the ultimate disclosure of the secret, expecting a happy surprise whenever she might penetrate the barrier of death.

Social Issues in Literature

Contemporary Perspectives on Death and Dying

The Idea of "Stages" of Grief Is a Myth

Russell Friedman and John W. James

Russell Friedman and John W. James are the principal leaders of the Grief Recovery Institute in Sherman Oaks, California, and are the coauthors of three books on grieving.

Friedman and James refute a theory put forward in 1969 and widely accepted without question by the psychological community, that there are distinct stages that every dying person and every grieving person go through. These stages, in order, are denial, anger, bargaining, depression, and acceptance. Not until 2001 did grief counselors begin to question what the authors regard as a damaging insistence on these "stages" and proceed to counsel grieving people without reference to this theory that they contend is not based on scientific evidence. Extensive research showed that a grieving person almost never denies death; that "disbelief" is only used rhetorically; that shock only occurs with sudden death; and that anger is rare. Those who have lost loved ones naturally want to understand their feelings and how to deal with them, but people grieve in unique ways, and to force them into false stages does irreparable harm.

In 1969 the psychiatrist Elizabeth Kübler-Ross wrote one of the most influential books in the history of psychology, *On Death and Dying*. It exposed the heartless treatment of terminally-ill patients prevalent at the time. On the positive side, it altered the care and treatment of dying people. On the negative side, it postulated the now-infamous five *stages of dy-*

Russell Friedman and John W. James, "The Myth of Stages of Dying and Grief," *Skeptic*, vol. 14, 2008, pp. 37–41.

ing—Denial, Anger, Bargaining, Depression, and Acceptance (DABDA), so annealed in culture that most people can recite them by heart. . . .

Refuting the Stages of Grief Theory

Many people have contested the validity of the stages of dying, but here we are more concerned with the supposed *stages of grief* which derived from the stages of dying. As professional grief recovery specialists, we contend that the theory of the stages of grief has done more harm than good to grieving people. Having co-authored three books on the impact of death, divorce, and other losses, and having worked directly with over 100,000 grieving people during the past 30 years, our reasons for disputing the stages of grief theory are predicated on the horror stories we've heard from thousands of grieving people who've told us how they'd been harmed by them. . . .

We're not sure why Kübler-Ross felt compelled to convert her observations from the interviews [she did with dying people] into stages. Possibly she believed that what she heard in her interviews with dying people was actually stages that needed to be quantified, or perhaps she simply attempted to put a scientific face on anecdotal evidence.

On February 21, 2007, *The Journal of the American Medical Association (JAMA)* published the results of the *Yale Bereavement Study (YBS): An Empirical Examination of the Stage Theory of Grief.* The YBS evaluated a hodge-podge of alleged stages. It starts with the assumption that *stages of grief* exist, and then attempts to use that assumption to prove that they do. However, the existence of stages has never been established as fact. The results appeared to confirm some stages, negate others, and reposition their order and value. We cannot give any credence to the YBS because its premises and conclusions are flawed. But, since the study's own language perpetuates the myth that stages of grief even exist, we'll use it to make our case. . . .

Prior to publication of her famous book, Kübler-Ross hypothesized the Five Stages of Receiving Catastrophic News, but in the text she renamed them the Five Stages of Dying or Five Stages of Death. That led to the later, improper shift to *stages of grief*. Had she stuck with the phrase *catastrophic news*, perhaps the mythology of stages wouldn't have emerged and grievers wouldn't be encouraged to try to fit their emotions into non-existent stages.

Adding irony to the stages debacle, Kübler-Ross' final book, *On Grief and Grieving*, is subtitled, *Finding The Meaning Of Grief Through The Five Stages Of Loss*. Confusingly, inside the book they're called the Five Stages of Grief. *Stages of loss* conveniently fit the new book on grief and confirmed the chameleon-like capacity of the word *stages* to arbitrarily mean whatever Kübler-Ross or anyone else wants it to mean. . . .

As we refute the stages, we'll address the most commonly used stages and point out how they have the potential to harm grieving people.

Some Elements of Stage One . . .

In our thousands of interactions with grieving people we have never found one person who was in denial that a loss had occurred. We ask, "What happened?" They say, "My mother died." There's no denial that someone died. We've had a few people tell us someone died and then say, "I'm in denial." We ask, "Do you mean the person isn't dead?" They say, "No, but I've heard 'denial' is the first stage of grief." . . .

In cases of sudden, unexpected deaths, it's possible that upon receiving the news, a surviving family member may go into emotional shock, during which time they're in a suspended state, totally removed from events in the real world. This response is rare and doesn't last very long. Most deaths are at the end of a long-term illness or of old age, and don't produce shock in the survivors. However, there are books that maintain that shock is a standard stage of grief. There is no evidence to support that idea. . . .

Numbness is one of the most common physiological responses to a grief-producing event. . . .

Grief related numbness is the result of an overload of emotional energy in reaction to a death. Many grievers report numbness as intermittent in the immediate aftermath of a death, which usually gives way to a lack of focus or limited concentration. However, numbness is not a stage, nor is the inability to concentrate. . . .

The Possible Harm Caused by Insistence on Stages

Time can't heal emotional wounds, but the word "stage" implies that time is a component. The suggestion to grievers that they're in a stage of denial or disbelief can freeze them into inaction. They bury their feelings waiting for time to make that stage pass. Later they're liable to be diagnosed with "complicated bereavement" and put on psychotropic drugs, which make it difficult or impossible for them to access the emotions they've buried. . . .

Many grievers tell us that a mental or medical health professional "strongly suggested" they were in the *denial* stage, when all they'd said was that they were having some difficulty since Mom died. Even after reiterating they were clear that Mom had died, the therapist insisted they were in denial, which created a breach of trust and safety. The grievers terminated therapy after one or two ineffective sessions, and left their grief unattended. We believe those professionals overlooked a cardinal rule of helping grievers, which is: "Hear what your client is telling you, as opposed to having your own agenda."

When an elderly loved one dies at the end of a long-term illness, there's usually no anger in those left behind. Along with feelings of sadness, there may be a sense of relief that the suffering is over. Things do happen relevant to a death that can make us angry: anger at a disease or God; anger at doctors or hospitals or the drunk driver who killed our loved one; even anger at loved ones who didn't take good care of themselves, or who took their own lives. But anger is not a universal feeling when someone important to us dies, and therefore is not a stage. . . .

When *anger* is perceived as a stage, there are no actions the griever can take to end it. They must stay angry as long it lasts or as long as they're alive. As we said, stages imply that time is an element, so when time fails to end that stage, people re-create and re-live anger for years. Staying angry can have dangerous consequences, causing people to damage relationships, lose jobs, and worse, affect their health or restrict their will to live. . . .

Grievers repeatedly tell us the same scenario about *anger* as about *denial*. They report that a mental or medical health professional "planted" the idea they were in a stage of anger, when nothing they'd said would indicate that this was true. . . .

The death of a long-term spouse creates an incalculable amount of emotional energy. Those feelings are often accompanied by an overwhelming sense of missing the person and wanting the familiarity of their presence back. Missing someone who has been a constant part of your life for decades is normal and to be expected. Again, calling it a stage [bargaining or yearning] suggests a time frame, causing them to wait for that stage to end which adds exponentially to their grief.

We're going to address *depression* in greater detail than the other alleged stages because it carries with it a great deal of confusion and potential danger for grieving people. Here is a list of reactions common to grievers that are also symptoms of clinical depression:

- inability to concentrate,
- disturbance of sleeping patterns,
- upheaval of eating patterns,
- roller coaster of emotions,
- lack of energy. . . .

It is normal for grievers to experience a lowered level of emotional and physical energy, which is neither clinical depression nor a stage. But when people believe depression is a stage that defines their sad feelings, they become trapped by the belief that after the passage of some time the stage will magically end. While waiting for the depression to lift, they take no actions that might help them. If and when they seek professional help, they use the self-diagnosis of depression to describe themselves.

When medical or psychological professionals hear grievers diagnose themselves as depressed, they often reflexively confirm that diagnosis and prescribe treatment with psychotropic drugs. The pharmaceutical companies which manufacture those drugs have a vested interest in sustaining the idea that grief-related depression is clinical, so their marketing supports the continuation of that belief.

The question of drug treatment for grief was addressed in the *National Comorbidity Survey.* "Criteria For Depression Are Too Broad Researchers Say—Guidelines May Encompass Many Who Are Just Sad." That headline trumpeted the survey's results, which observed more than 8,000 subjects and revealed that as many as 25% of grieving people diagnosed as depressed and placed on antidepressant drugs, are *not* clinically depressed. The study indicated they would benefit far more from supportive therapies that could keep them from developing full-blown depression. . . .

One definition of stages cannot fit all people, or all relationships—in fact we don't think they fit anybody. For example, an 85-year old woman whose spouse of 62 years has died reports a different emotional picture about her life and response to that death, than does a 62-year old woman whose 85-year old father has died. Both involve 62-year relationships, but the idea that there could be a stage of acceptance applicable to both is illogical. . . .

If there are no typical responses to loss and no typical losses, and not everyone goes through them or in order, how can there possibly be stages that universally represent people's reactions to loss? The fact is, no study has ever established that stages of grief actually exist, and what are defined as such can't be called stages. Grief is the normal and natural emotional response to loss. Stage theories put grieving people in conflict with their emotional reactions to losses that affect them. No matter how much people want to create simple, iron clad guidelines for the human emotions of grief, there are no stages of grief that fit every person or relationship.

The Death of a Loved One Can Lead to Renewal

Darlene F. Cross

Darlene F. Cross is a marriage and family therapist with a long-term focus on grief and loss cases.

In this excerpt Cross describes the trauma that led her to specialize in dying and grief. That trauma was facing the impending death of her mother, who unexpectedly began having severe heart attacks. Like Emily Dickinson, Cross goes into shock and her actions become mechanical, after she receives the news that her mother has been taken to the hospital in an ambulance. She goes into denial, refusing to believe the doctor who tells her that her mother is dying. Part of the trial of facing her mother's death is carrying out her mother's death directive that she not be placed on life support. In the airplane, traveling to her mother's bedside, and in her mother's room, she speaks of death's unreality and her own confusion. The morning of the second day, looking at her dead mother, she thinks that she is seeing not only her mother's death but her own.

The obnoxious phone jarred me awake too early on the morning of December 24, 1994. I figured it had to be someone calling from the Eastern Time Zone because it happened so often and was always annoying. I remember swearing to myself when I moved back to the east I would never be so inconsiderate of Pacific Time Zone people again.

The call was from an Ohio relative letting me know she had received a call from a local hospital. She said my mother had been taken there by ambulance, but she had no idea why. Hospital? Ambulance?

I was baffled. I'd spoken with Mom on the phone the previous evening. She had taken the day off work to finish last-minute Christmas shopping and said she didn't feel well. Her back had been bothering her and treatment had not relieved the discomfort, but there were no other apparent issues with her health. We were both tired from holiday stress and agreed to get some rest. I promised to check on her in the morning, and we said, "Good-night." I couldn't even guess how she could be in the hospital, via ambulance no less, only hours later.

I quickly called long distance to the hospital, expecting to get a volunteer giving me some generic status report. Instead, I was immediately connected to the attending physician. What on earth was happening?

The Shock of Crisis

The physician was kind, but direct and to the point. She informed me my mother had called for an ambulance, let the Emergency Medical Technicians into her home, and proceeded to have a massive heart attack. She said they "lost her" in the ambulance on the way to the hospital, succeeded in reviving her, and she'd had a second attack that had destroyed the main valve in her heart. She told me my mother was not going to live.

Well, that was just absurd. This had to be some awful mistake. I just talked to Mom and, except for the back ache, she was fine. My mother was young, only 69 years old, and came from a long line of strong women who live and lived forever. She'd never even been in the hospital, other than to give birth decades before. Her own mother as of this writing is 102 and pretty healthy for an old lady. I was taking the situation seriously, but clearly the physician had to be horribly mistaken.

Being the dutiful daughter who loved her mother very much, I was faced with my first choice. If there was any truth to what I was being told, I needed to be my mother's voice as

I had promised to do. Would I honor her wishes made so clear to me in the past, or would I choose what I wanted which was not to lose my mother? In my mind, there was no choice as I said, "My mother did not want any heroic measures ever taken on her behalf. I do not want her to be placed on life support." There, I said it.

Ignorance isn't always bliss. Without hesitation, the physician informed me that not only was my mother already on life support, but that if it was disconnected, she would immediately die. I was then slapped with my next choice when she asked, "What do you want?"

The Overwhelming Decision

What do I want? What do I *want*? I want to go to the bathroom since I was just so rudely jerked awake! I want some caffeine, a whole vat of caffeine! I want to go back to sleep and end this awful nightmare, wake up and start this day over again! This was not happening.

As calmly as I could, I told the physician to do whatever tests she needed to do so we could make a fully-informed decision. I told her while she completed all the tests, I would be on an airplane to get there as fast as I could, and allow the family time to gather. She agreed but followed with the warning, "Don't expect your mom to be alive when you get here." This woman sure wasn't cutting me any slack. I'd say I was speechless, but I told her the only thing I knew to say, the only thing I knew to be true. "She'll wait for me."

I went into achievement-oriented auto pilot. Shock really does come in handy sometimes. I made arrangements to vanish instantly with no idea when I would return. I slung clothes into a suitcase and froze when the next choice gave me a sour look at my situation. Did I pack an outfit appropriate for a funeral, my mother's funeral? Knowing the one thing my mother was most proud of in her entire life was her children, I made my wardrobe choice for her. I packed an outfit I was to wear only one more time.

I won't attempt to describe the flight from Vegas to Cleveland; I'm not sure I could. Nothing was real. I got into my rental car and somehow an hour later walked into the hospital just before midnight.

I had no idea what to expect. It was so hushed, so quiet. There were Christmas decorations everywhere. I tiptoed into the Coronary Care Unit and was amazed when I was happily greeted by multiple medical people calling me by name, saying they knew I'd just flown in from Las Vegas, talking as if they'd known me forever. My mother was alive. They took me into see her, and there were those big brown eyes that just sparkled the minute she saw me. My mother waited for me.

I visited for only the few minutes allowed and left the hospital to head for my home away from home, my aunt and uncle's house. Amazingly, driving through a city I was born, raised and lived in for 30 years, I got lost, really lost. I'm still not sure exactly how I finally arrived at my destination.

Christmas Day was spent with family, short visits in and out with Mom who actually seemed to be doing better. The staff was encouraging as the day went on, in my mind confirming my gene pool theory as fact—we are strong women who live forever. We got the encouraging news that Mom would be moved out of CCU to a regular room in the morning. Feeling hopeful and a little more relaxed, we all realized how hungry and exhausted we were and went to enjoy a late holiday feast while Mom rested.

Death Gets Too Close

Then, it happened again. I had barely fallen asleep, complete with a too full stomach, when the hateful ring of the phone woke the household in the very early morning hours of December 26. It was the hospital. They said, "Come now."

Some day I may forgive my uncle for driving so slow, for his determination to get us to the hospital safely on snowy roads. Half way there, I knew it no longer mattered. I knew the moment my mother was gone.

I jumped out of the car before it stopped in the hospital parking lot and I ran. The elevator doors opened for me almost as if by magic, and the staff was waiting for me as I walked off. They shared the news that was not news. They said things I didn't understand, things that really didn't matter anymore, anyway. Their words were a garbled mess and all I could do was nod my head, indicating I understood when I didn't understand at all.

I walked into the room alone. There were those same brown eyes, only now looking anything but alive. I knew I should close them, but I just couldn't do it. I touched her arm that was cool but still warm at the same time. It was immediately clear to me—this was not my mother. This was my mother's body. It looked so small. I didn't know it was possible to hurt so much, or how I could go on if it didn't stop. I didn't think I would ever be able to breathe again.

I am fortunate to look like my mother, but in that moment the similarity brought anything but comfort. I was seeing my own death on top of my mother's. I realized how little time I really have left, and how precious every minute really is. My own life review flew through my mind with clarity I had never experienced before, and my New Normal began to form. I vowed in that moment to experience every single emotion in honor of my amazing mother and this tremendous loss. Then I went to throw up. . . .

Renewal After Death

It will come as no surprise that I began to work with grief and loss cases early in my new career, or that I never stopped. I launched my solo private practice in 1998, and I love my work as much or more today as I did then. Today, I define what success means to me instead of allowing others to do it for me. Today, the definition of success starts with happiness. Today, I am successful.

I still miss my mom all these years later. I have never completely run out of tears, but I did work through the pain, and I did breathe again. The sadness slowly faded and was replaced with an acceptance that allows me to have her with me always. She was never a big fan of therapy, so I wonder what she would think of her daughter, the psychotherapist. I wonder what she would say about her six amazing adult grandchildren or her adorable four little great grandchildren.

Facing Death Puts Life into Perspective

Randy Pausch

Randy Pausch was a professor of computer science and design at Carnegie Mellon University. His book The Last Lecture *became a* New York Times *best seller.*

In the following viewpoint Pausch, who spent the last several months of his life battling pancreatic cancer, talks about his experience facing death. He was curious and positively involved with the treatment he received. The day came when he and his family were to find out if the radical surgery, chemotherapy, and radiation had made changes in his prognosis. In the examining room, after the nurse had left, he and his wife realized that the results of his tests were visible on the computer. Alone in the room, they discovered that his situation was hopeless and began to cry together. Though he was stunned by the news, he did not give in to despair but remained somewhat scientifically interested in his condition. He confronted the new reality of a brief life and decided to live intensely in the moment, enjoying life with his loved ones to the utmost. Pausch died at the age of forty-seven.

My medical odyssey began in the summer of 2006, when I first felt slight, unexplained pain in my upper abdomen. Later, jaundice set in, and my doctors suspected I had hepatitis. That turned out to be wishful thinking. CT scans revealed I had pancreatic cancer, and it would take me just ten seconds on Google to discover how bad this news was. Pancreatic cancer has the highest mortality rate of any cancer; half of those diagnosed with it die within six months, and 96 percent die within five years. . . .

The Urge to Avoid One's Own Death

I told doctors that I'd be willing to endure anything in their surgical arsenal, and I'd swallow anything in their medicine cabinet, because I had an objective: I wanted to be alive as long as possible for Jai and the kids. At my first appointment with Pittsburgh surgeon Herb Zeh, I said: "Let's be clear. My goal is to be alive and on your brochure in ten years." . . .

In August, it was time for my quarterly check-in back at MD Anderson. Jai and I flew to Houston for the appointment, leaving the kids with a babysitter back home. We treated the trip like something of a romantic getaway. We even went to a giant water park the day before—I know, my idea of a romantic getaway—and I rode the speed slide, grinning all the way down.

Then, on August 15, 2007, a Wednesday, Jai and I arrived at MD Anderson to go over the results of my latest CT scans with my oncologist, Robert Wolff. We were ushered into an examining room, where a nurse asked a few routine questions. "Any changes in your weight, Randy? Are you still taking the same medications?" Jai took note of the nurse's happy, sing-song voice as she left, how she cheerily said, "OK, the doctor will be in to see you soon," as she closed the door behind her.

The examining room had a computer in it, and I noticed that the nurse hadn't logged out; my medical records were still up on the screen. I know my way around computers, of course, but this required no hacking at all. My whole chart was right there.

"Shall we have a look-see?" I said to Jai. I felt no qualms at all about what I was about to do. After all, these were my records.

The Stark Truth of Death's Eminence

I clicked around and found my blood-work report. There were 30 obscure blood values, but I knew the one I was looking for: CA 19-9—the tumor marker. When I found it, the number was a horrifying 208. A normal value is under 37. I studied it for just a second.

"It's over," I said to Jai. "My goose is cooked."

"What do you mean?" she asked.

I told her the CA 19-9 value. She had educated herself enough about cancer treatment to know that 208 indicated metastasis: a death sentence. "It's not funny," she said. "Stop joking around."

I then pulled up my CT scans on the computer and started counting. "One, two, three, four, five, six . . ."

I could hear the panic in Jai's voice. "Don't tell me you're counting tumors," she said. I couldn't help myself. I kept counting aloud. "Seven, eight, nine, ten . . ." I saw it all. The cancer had metastasized to my liver.

Jai walked over to the computer, saw everything clearly with her own eyes, and fell into my arms. We cried together. And that's when I realized there was no box of tissues in the room. I had just learned I would soon die, and in my inability to stop being rationally focused, I found myself thinking: "Shouldn't a room like this, at a time like this, have a box of Kleenex? Wow, that's a glaring operational flaw."

There was a knock on the door. Dr. Wolff entered, a folder in his hand. He looked from Jai to me to the CT scans on the computer, and he knew what had just happened. I decided to just be preemptive. "We know," I said.

By that point, Jai was almost in shock, crying hysterically. I was sad, too, of course, and yet I was also fascinated by the way in which Dr. Wolff went about the grim task before him. The doctor sat next to Jai to comfort her. Calmly, he explained to her that he would no longer be working to save my life. "What we're trying to do," he said, "is extend the time Randy

Hundreds of stuffed Tiggers adorn the seats for Carnegie Mellon University's memorial service (2008) in honor of professor and author Randy Pausch, whose famous last lecture, given when he knew he would soon die, urged people to embrace the childlike wonder represented by the character Tigger in A.A. Milne's The House at Pooh Corner. © AP Images/Gene J. Puskar.

has left so he can have the highest quality of life. That's because, as things now stand, medical science doesn't have anything to offer him to keep him alive for a normal life span."

"Wait, wait, wait," Jai said. "You're telling me that's it? Just like that, we've gone from 'we're going to fight this' to 'the battle is over'? What about a liver transplant?"

No, the doctor said, not once the metastasis occurs. He talked about using palliative chemo—treatment that's not intended to be curative, but could ease symptoms, possibly buying a few months—and about finding ways to keep me comfortable and engaged in life as the end approached.

A Sense of Detachment

The whole horrible exchange was surreal for me. Yes, I felt stunned and bereft for myself and especially for Jai, who couldn't stop crying. But a strong part of me remained in Randy Scientist Mode, collecting facts and quizzing the doctor about options. At the same time, there was another part of me that was utterly engaged in the theater of the moment. I felt incredibly impressed—awed really—by the way Dr. Wolff was giving the news to Jai. I thought to myself: "Look at how he's doing this. He's obviously done this so many times before, and he's good at it. He's carefully rehearsed, and yet everything is still so heartfelt and spontaneous."

I took note of how the doctor rocked back in his chair and closed his eyes before answering a question, almost as if that was helping him think harder. I watched the doctor's body posture, the way he sat next to Jai. I found myself almost detached from it all, thinking: "He isn't putting his arm around her shoulder. I understand why. That would be too presumptuous. But he's leaning in, his hand on her knee. Boy, he's good at this."

I wished every medical student considering oncology could see what I was seeing. I watched Dr. Wolff use semantics to phrase whatever he could in a positive light. When we asked, "How long before I die?" he answered, "You probably have three to six months of good health." That reminded me of my time at Disney. Ask Disney World workers: "What time does the park close?" They're supposed to answer: "The park is *open* until 8 p.m."

In a way, I felt an odd sense of relief. For too many tense months, Jai and I had been waiting to see if and when the tumors would return. Now here they were, a full army of them. The wait was over. Now we could move on to dealing with whatever came next.

The Short Life Needs to Be Lived

At the end of the meeting, the doctor hugged Jai and shook my hand, and Jai and I walked out together, into our new reality.

Leaving the doctor's office, I thought about what I'd said to Jai in the water park in the afterglow of the speed slide.

"Even if the scan results are bad tomorrow," I had told her, "I just want you to know that it feels great to be alive, and to be here today, alive with you. Whatever news we get about the scans, I'm not going to die when we hear it. I won't die the next day, or the day after that, or the day after that. So today, right now, well this is a wonderful day. And I want you to know how much I'm enjoying it."

I thought about that, and about Jai's smile.

I knew then. That's the way the rest of my life would need to be lived.

Western Approaches to Death Are Unnatural

Maurice Abitbol

Maurice Abitbol is a practicing physician at Jamaica Hospital in New York and a professor at the State University of New York.

Abitbol suggests a more humane way for contemporary society to contemplate death. This he does by pointing out the difference between Western and Eastern philosophies. Part of the problem with the West's current reaction to death is that after years of a religion-instilled horror of death, medical science began coldly dictating the terms of dying: prolonging pain and using unnatural methods to keep patients alive for a few weeks against their will. Yet science does not and cannot solve the mystery of the afterlife. Now a paucity of anything remotely spiritual considered in decisions and directions for the dying has created a vacuum. Yet members of Eastern cultures find death neither frightening nor confusing. The dying are given death with dignity and the opportunity to choose pain control and euthanasia. Hindus, for example, do not interfere with the process of death unless the dying person wishes it.

Historical analysis gives us insights into how and why we believe what we do about death. Without this historical perspective, we jump to conclusions—often false conclusions. It helps to understand that our current approach to dying and death evolved out of a series of events and beliefs, and that what evolved is not necessarily the right approach.

Knowledge provides us with a broader frame of reference in which to think about a situation. When we remove the mystery from our current practices regarding the dead, we can look at these practices more objectively. We can also become more open-minded about alternatives to the status quo.

Let's begin our historical analysis by considering the five different ways people view life after death and how these perspectives evolved. . . .

Six Types of Afterlife

People think about the afterlife in strikingly different ways. Here are the six most common perceptions:

1. *No life or existence after death.* Atheism endorses this notion, and it has gained many adherents over the years. Agnostics or even those who have some religious affiliation may lean toward this view.

2. *Memory after death.* As we've discussed earlier, the notion of a persistent memory is one in which we remain in the minds of those who have known us, especially our family, friends and colleagues. Some leave a lasting memory represented by earthly accomplishments while a few achieve a larger measure of fame.

3. *Existence of life beyond earth in terrestrial terms.* We are physically transported to a religious paradise or hell. This viewpoint is losing favor in most religions and countries; the idea of a cosmic existence is usually integrated with this paradisial place.

4. *Cosmic existence.* A pure and abstract existence, detached from one's body as well as from space, time, familiar surroundings and even consciousness. While on earth, we can prepare for this new kind of existence, especially in old age, by learning to separate from our attachments and learn to perceive the beyond.

5. *Reincarnation.* Our soul was in someone else before our birth and will go to someone else after we die. This concept is more common than one might imagine and is

not necessarily religious in nature. Some cultures believe they are reincarnated in their children while others believe they come back as animals.

6. *Blocking the subject.* Some people become very nervous when the subject is discussed and prefer not to talk about it.

The Historical Shaping of Our Perceptions

Until the Middle Ages ended and the Renaissance began (end of the 15th century), civilized people had an almost uniform belief in life after death. God, heaven and hell and the idea of death as a passage from one condition to the next were widely accepted except for a few intellectual skeptics. While the concept of an afterlife varied among different religious groups, it was always present and automatically accepted.

Before Christianity, the belief was that the body and soul together were transferred to an afterlife. There was, therefore, respect for the dead body which was considered the carrier even after death. Ceremonies revolved around this belief, perhaps the most well-known ones being the embalming of the corpse and the construction of the pyramids for the Pharaohs of ancient Egypt. With the advent of Christianity, people began viewing the body and soul as separate entities. The biological demands of the body (food, sex, etc.) were considered handicaps for the movement of the soul. Although people enjoyed themselves during their lifetimes, this enjoyment was considered almost sinful. Death was nothing more than the liberation of the soul from the body and the soul went to heaven (or hell or purgatory). The Christian dying ceremony represented the detachment of the soul from the body and all of its sinful pleasures. The dead body was no longer viewed as a carrier and became less important. It was nothing more than a reminder, a symbol, of the departed person.

Until the end of the Middle Ages, each event in the universe was considered a divine miracle. Everything was a miraculous event: day and night, sunrise and sunset, the seasons, plants, animals, life, and birth. Given this perspective, even death possessed a miraculous aura. To question whether death might simply be a sleep from which one did not awake was almost inconceivable. Without a scientific explanation, death and other events were elevated far beyond the status to which scientific thought reduced them. Given the miracles all around people, being religious was as natural as breathing. Religious leaders didn't spend their time attempting to convince people of the existence of God; everyone knew it to be true. Instead, the priests were involved in teaching a specific form of belief and a specific way of life according to the will of a specific God. The adversaries of a religion were not atheists or nonbelievers but those who deviated from the specific teaching of a given religion and altered its well-delineated dogma. To convert someone to a religion was not to convert a nonbeliever to a believer but to transfer someone from the dogma of one religion to the dogma of another. It should be noted that the term, evangelize, originally meant to substitute Christianity for Paganism; it connoted change of religions.

In Ancient History, Dying Was an Act of God

Throughout ancient history, there were a few isolated rebellions against these beliefs such as the rational thinking of the Greek philosophers. But the all-powerful church quickly put down these rebellions. Tools such as the Inquisition also discouraged any deviation from the norm. Even medicine was under the authority of the church and some medical schools of the Middle Ages were run by the clergy. Doctors were not responsible for death and people died because God called them to join Him. Unless it was an obvious criminal act (stabbing, poisoning, etc.) death, specifically a slow, disease-induced death, was always an act of God.

It was only at the end of the Middle Ages that doubt about an afterlife started to creep in. This transformation in thought, which started at the beginning of the 16th century, was widespread by the 19th century, at least in the Western World.

Image from the Egyptian Book of the Dead, an ancient funerary text containing spells to guide the dead person through the underworld and into the afterlife. © AP Images/North Wind Picture Archives.

Though there are still people who believe in an afterlife, doubt always exists. Religious leaders today, unlike those before the 16th century, labor mightily to convince people of divine existence. This change says a lot about how our beliefs have been transformed.

Death in the Age of Doubt

We've also become very skeptical of miracles, and religious belief has a rather narrow connotation, meaning that one believes in some kind of modus operandi in the universe that has no physical or scientific explanation. A religious person believes in events that are in opposition to the laws of a biological and physical world. It's rare today to find some event that is not scientifically explained and which would imply a divine (or demonic) presence.

The change from belief to non-belief probably took a couple of centuries, and it was catalyzed by scientific explanations for an increasing number of previously unexplained phenomenon. Everything in the universe, such as sunrise and sunset and rain or drought, received a scientific explanation instead of being accepted as divine miracles. The body started to be better understood in terms of its physiology and pathology. Death was understood in terms of physiological failures that could sometimes be corrected. As skepticism about afterlife continued to creep in, death became a horror and discussing it became frightening because it signified the end of everything. Not only was it frightening to elderly people but to anyone as they aged. Even the clergy started to talk less about death and only spoke of absolution and heaven (much less of hell). They didn't have answers to those dreaded questions about death; it was better to keep those questions buried in the subconscious than allow them to surface. I imagine the clergy themselves were too frightened and confused by their own doubts and were eager to drop the subject of death.

The Doctor, Not God, Controls Life and Death

As doctors gradually freed themselves from the powerful grip of the Church, they had more opportunities to use real science to investigate causes of disease and determine treatment. Instead of relying on prayers, they could put their science to work. At first, this was a radical departure from tradition, since doctors were burned at the stake in the Middle Ages for separating medicine from religion.

But the opportunities afforded by this new medical freedom also came with a price: It was no longer God's will if the treatment failed; rather, it was the doctor's failure. Now the doctor, not God, became the maker of life and death. Over time, doctors became the managers of death and dying, a role the clergy was more than eager to turn over to them. When someone was dying, a doctor was called before or even instead of the priest. Unfortunately, doctors didn't have as much experience dealing with dying people that the clergy had developed over the centuries. The clergy had been carefully taught, during their priesthood training, how to interact with the dying and their skilled manner was always a comfort. Doctors lacked this training. Even more troublesome, doctors weren't allowed to talk about afterlife since it was unscientific, unproved and irrational. For doctors as well as patients, death had become a dreaded subject, one that was difficult to discuss at all.

To talk or not to talk about death, that was the question and the dilemma facing doctors. For most the 17th, 18th and 19th centuries, doctors didn't resolve this dilemma. Instead, they avoided the subject as much as possible. Without the training or experience, they managed the deaths of their patients uncertainly and inconsistently.

Medical, Not Religious, Dogma

By the beginning of the 20th century, however, doctors took a new approach: They decided to rebel against death and fight it until the bitter end. This rebellion would have been considered sacrilegious during the Middle Ages. Today, however, it has become medical dogma. While extending life is a noble goal, it ceases to be noble when the life that is extended is filled with suffering. Extending life at any cost has more in common with the tortures of the Inquisition than the wise and compassionate use of modern science.

Through gerontology, doctors have learned to extend life into very old age, resulting in a significant percentage of senior citizens who are completely bedridden and mentally deficient. This country now has 50,000 centenarians, a few healthy but most suffering from varying degrees of physical or mental defects. Using science to sustain the lives of terminally ill and elderly people is a worthy goal if the following criteria are kept in mind:

1. Patients should not be used as guinea pigs to test new or experimental treatments.

2. The life-extending treatments should not be motivated by our fear of death.

3. Treatment should be in response to the patient's desire to be kept alive rather than someone else's wish (or fear).

Unfortunately, these criteria are often ignored as the entire healthcare industry—doctors, nurses, administrators, hospitals, HMOs—has joined the fight against death. Advances in medical care, medical technology, pharmacology, and medical equipment have been aimed at extended life. In this zealous quest to add hours or days to a person's life, what gets lost are quality of life issues. Historical progress in medicine may be easier to measure in quantitative terms—in the amount of time we can extend lives through modern medicine—but the true measure is improving the quality of life. . . .

How the Medical Profession Took over the Mortuary Function

The price of consciousness and of superior thinking that characterizes humans is the awareness that one is alive as well as that one is dying. Since the dawn of mankind, humans have struggled unsuccessfully with how to die and what happens to us after death. The relief and comfort offered by religion was temporary and is now vanishing. Almost by default, the medical profession has taken over this role of reliever and comforter. In reality, doctors have no training whatsoever to deal with these issues. They are taught how to save lives and not how to help people when they're dying. If doctors are going to perform this role effectively—and I am not sure they should—then they need special training and a completely different attitude.

How the medical profession got involved in the pre-mortuary and mortuary function is a mystery of the evolution of medicine into which historians of the next generation will try to delve. The most mystifying aspect is that today it has become so natural that no one finds anything mysterious about it.

Presently, when the question of possible death arises, when someone is dying, when someone presents any problem while dying, when someone is pronounced dead, when the news is to be announced to the family, when it comes to the family's bereavement, and even the administrative papers associated with death (death certificate), the medical profession is asked to handle everything. Not only is it a mystery to me that everyone finds this medical function natural, but that the doctor also finds it natural, and most often the doctor "does something." From a medical point of view this means nothing, since the patient dies anyway. Under these conditions, to do something often ends up being harmful.

For Further Discussion

1. What events in Emily Dickinson's life may have contributed to her fixation on death? See Chronology, and essays by Ruth Miller, Alfred Habegger, and John Cody.

2. Discuss Dickinson's view of death as the solving of a mystery and ultimate freedom. See Clark Griffith, David Porter, Joan Kirby, Wendy Martin, and Jane Donahue Eberwein.

3. Examine the personification of death in Dickinson's poems. See Thomas H. Johnson.

4. Critics disagree about whether Dickinson believed in life after death. Debate this topic making reference to her poems. See Robert Weisbuch, Martin, Patrick J. Keane, and Eberwein.

5. Much attention is given to the grieving of the dead's loved ones. Do you find elements common to Dickinson's reference to grieving and contemporary works? See Griffith, Paul Ferlazzo, Eberwein, Russell Friedman and John W. James, and Darlene F. Cross.

6. The persistence of death causes many to dismiss the traditional view of death as romantic as well as the idea that God is good. Discuss this with reference to Dickinson's poems. Also see Bettina L. Knapp, Kirby, and Keane.

For Further Reading

Emily Dickinson, *Dickinson: Selected Poems and Commentaries*. Ed. Helen Vendler. Cambridge, MA: Belknap Press of Harvard University Press, 2010.

———, *Emily Dickinson's Letters*. New York: Alfred A. Knopf, 2011.

———, *Open Me Carefully: Emily Dickinson's Intimate Letter to Susan Huntington Dickinson*. Eds. Ellen Louise Hart and Martha Nell Smith. Ashfield, MA: Paris Press, 1998.

Ralph Waldo Emerson, *Essays: First and Second Series*. New York: Library of America, 2010.

———, *Poems: A Variorum Edition*. Cambridge, MA: Belknap Press of Harvard University Press, 2011.

John Keats, *The Poems of John Keats*. Ed. Jack Stillinger. Cambridge, MA: Harvard University Press, 1978. (See "When I Have Fears That I May Cease to Be," "Sonnet to Sleep," "Ode to a Nightingale," and "Ode on Melancholy.")

Edgar Allan Poe, *The Collected Letters of Edgar Allan Poe*. Staten Island, NY: Gordeau Press, 2008.

———, *Great Tales and Poems*. New York: Vintage Books, 2009.

Tom Pomplum, ed., *Gothic Classics*. Mount Horeb, WI: Eureka Productions, 2007.

Walt Whitman, *Song of Myself, and Other Poems*. Berkeley, CA: Counterpoint, 2010.

Bibliography

Books

Charles R. Anderson	*Emily Dickinson's Poetry: Stairway of Surprise.* New York: Holt, Rinehart and Winston, 1960.
Richard Chase	*Emily Dickinson.* New York: William Sloane, 1951.
Joan Didion	*The Year of Magical Thinking.* New York: Alfred A. Knopf, 2005.
Joanne F. Diehl	*Dickinson and the Romantic Imagination.* Princeton, NJ: Princeton University Press, 1981.
Denis Donoghue	*Emily Dickinson.* Minneapolis: University of Minneapolis Press, 1966.
Thomas W. Ford	*Heaven Beguiles the Tired: Death in the Poetry of Emily Dickinson.* Tuscaloosa: University of Alabama Press, 1966.
Albert J. Gelpi	*Emily Dickinson: The Mind of the Poet.* Cambridge, MA: Harvard University Press, 1966.
Salamatullah Khan	"Emily Dickinson on Death," in *Indian Response to American Literature.* Ed. C.D. Narasimhaiah. New Delhi: U.S. Educational Foundation in India, 1967.

Inder Nath Kher   *The Landscape of Absence: Emily Dickinson's Poetry.* New Haven, CT: Yale University Press, 1974.

Jay Leyda   *The Years and Hours of Emily Dickinson.* New Haven, CT: Yale University Press, 1960.

James McIntosh   *Nimble Believing: Dickinson and the Unknown.* Ann Arbor: University of Michigan Press, 2000.

Ruth Miller   *The Poetry of Emily Dickinson.* Middletown, CT: Wesleyan University Press, 1968.

Joyce Carol Oates   *A Widow's Story.* New York: HarperCollins, 2011.

Lawrence J. Schneiderman   *Embracing Our Mortality.* New York: Oxford University Press, 2008.

Richard B. Sewall   *The Life of Emily Dickinson.* Vols. I and II. New York: Farrar, Straus, and Giroux, 1974.

Martha N. Smith   *Rowing in Eden: Rereading Emily Dickinson.* Austin: University of Texas Press, 1992.

John Evangelist Walsh   *The Hidden Life of Emily Dickinson.* New York: Simon and Schuster, 1971.

Simone Weil   "The Love of God and Affliction," in *Waiting for God.* Trans. Emma Craufurd. New York: G. P. Putnam's Sons, 1951.

Periodicals

Virginia H. Adair "Dickinson's Death Is a Dialogue Between," *Explicator*, vol. 27, no. 7, 1969.

John Q. Anderson "The Funeral Procession in Dickinson's Poetry," *Emerson Society Journal*, no. 44, Third Quarter, 1977.

Martin Bickman "Kora in Heaven: Love and Death in the Poetry of Emily Dickinson," *Emily Dickinson Bulletin*, no. 32, 1977.

E. Miller Budick "Assignable Portion," *Dickinson Studies*, no. 36, 1979.

Jane Crosthwaite "Ride with Death," *American Transcendental Quarterly*, no. 42, Spring 1979.

Donald H. Cunningham "Emily Dickinson's 'I Heard a Fly Buzz,'" *American Notes and Queries*, vol. 6, no. 10, June 1968.

Edgar F. Daniels "Dickinson's 'As By the Dead We Love to Sit,'" *Explicator*, vol. 35, no. 2, Winter 1976.

Mario L. D'Avanzo "Emily Dickinson's Dying Eye," *Renascence*, vol. 19, no. 2, Winter 1967.

J. Chris Hackler and F. Charles Hiller "Family Consent to Orders Not to Resuscitate: Reconsidering Hospital Policy," *Journal of the American Medical Association*, vol. 264, no. 10, 1990.

Larry Oliver   "Apocalypse of Green," *Dickinson Studies*, no. 44, 1982.

John Rachel   "Probing the Final Mystery," *Dickinson Studies*, no. 39, 1981.

R.A. Sheffler   "Emily Dickinson's 'A Clock Stopped,'" *Massachusetts Studies in English*, vol. 1, no. 2, Fall 1967.

H. Taylor   "Withholding and Withdrawal of Life Support from the Critically Ill," *New England Journal of Medicine*, no. 322, 1990.

Index